About the Series

IDEAS IN PROGRESS is a commercially published series of working papers dealing with alternatives to industrial society. It is our belief that the ills and profound frustrations which have overtaken us are not merely due to industrial civilization's inadequate planning and faulty execution, but are caused by fundamental errors in our basic thinking about goals. This series is designed to question and rethink the underlying concepts of many of our institutions and to propose alternatives. Unless this is done soon society will undoubtedly create even greater injustices and inequalities than at present. It is to correct this trend that authors are invited to submit short texts of work in progress of interest not only to their colleagues but also to the general public. The series fosters direct contact between the author and the reader. It provides the author with the opportunity to give wide circulation to his draft while he is still developing an idea. It offers the reader an opportunity to participate critically in shaping this idea before it has taken on a definitive form.

Readers are invited to write directly to the author of the present volume at the following address:
Virginia Novarra, 12 St Edmund's Court, St Edmund's Terrace, London NW8 7QL.

THE PUBLISHERS

ABOUT THE AUTHOR

Virginia Novarra took her law degree at London University and began her career as a lawyer in the City of London. She then moved to the Port of London Authority where she worked on modernizing legislation and then managed their Central Services Department. In 1968 she was the first woman to be appointed a Principal Officer of the Port of London Authority. She then became an Assistant Secretary to the Committee of London Clearing Bankers and British Bankers Association (1970–73). During this time she was involved in high level committee work on an international scale. In 1974 she attended the London Business School for an Executive Programme which included finance, statistics and marketing. Since 1974 Virginia Novarra has worked as a Principal in the Civil Service, initially in the Department of Prices and was involved in advising ministers in the fields of price controls and commodity prices. From 1976–77 she was seconded for a special project to reform piece-rate systems in an engineering company. In 1977 she was elected chairman of the UNCTAD Iron Ore Conference in Geneva. She is currently in the team negotiating compensation under the Aircraft and Shipbuilding Industries Act.

She has contributed articles in the *Law Society Gazette* and *Solicitors' Journal*. She is a founder member of *Women's Report Collective,* an executive committee member of Women in Management and a former board member of International Advance of Women. She was made a Churchill Fellow in 1975, and is the originator of *Women's Who's Who, UK*.

Presently she is setting up an academic journal on women's employment with an international bias and is planning the establishment of a high level management development course for women.

WOMEN'S WORK, MEN'S WORK

To all the friends
in various parts of the world who have
given me data of all kinds
on equal employment opportunity
and kindred subjects –

and with special thanks
to Eileen, Joe and Sally,
who gave support and encouragement
while this book was being
written, of which the author
wishes to record her deep
appreciation

IDEAS IN PROGRESS

WOMEN'S WORK, MEN'S WORK

THE AMBIVALENCE OF EQUALITY

Virginia Novarra

MARION BOYARS

LONDON · BOSTON

First Published simultaneously in Great Britain
and the United States in 1980
by Marion Boyars Publishers Ltd.
18 Brewer Street, London W1R 4AS
and Marion Boyars Inc.
99 Main Street, Salem, New Hampshire 03079

Australian distribution by Thomas C. Lothian
4–12 Tattersalls Lane, Melbourne, Victoria 3000

British Library Cataloguing in Publication Data
Novarra, Virginia
    Women's work, men's work. – (Ideas in progress).
    1. Women's rights – History
    I. Title II. Series
    301.41'2'09   HQ1121   79–41252
        ISBN 0 7145 2680 0   cased edition
            0 7145 2681 9   paper edition
Library of Congress Catalog Card Number 79–67452

Printed in Great Britain by
Redwood Burn Limited
Trowbridge & Esher

CONTENTS

PREFACE   1

ANATOMY OF A FEMINIST – a personal foreword   7

1 WOMEN'S WORK AND MEN'S WORK   17
Women's work – What do we mean by work? –
Men's work – 'Women workers' and 'ladies of
leisure' – 'Work' is a system made by men for men –
Women's contribution, actual and potential

2 THEORY AND IDEOLOGY   53
Women have been ignored by the thinkers – political
theory and politicians' sexism – economics – Pigou –
growing preoccupation with women by economists
– economic theory still inadequate – sociology of
work – specialist studies of women's employment

3 THE WOMEN'S MOVEMENT   71
What happened after women 'won their rights' – the
lost generations – the women's movement in terms
of political theory – the women's movement today –
women's opposition to the movement – do men
have a part to play? – the women's movement and
employment issues

4 THE LABOUR MARKET TODAY   90
Women are the growth element in the labour force –
changes in employment of married women – women
worse hit by unemployment – women's narrow

range of occupations – pay and other conditions are not equal – women are not in a position to influence the future

5   ELIMINATING SEX-SEGREGATION IN   98
EMPLOYMENT
'Work' is already unisex technically – impediments to equal opportunity – governmental action for equal opportunity – equal opportunity laws – scope – procedure for dealing with complaints – beyond the individual case – publicity – the official agency – strategy for equal opportunity agencies – affirmative action

6   EQUAL OPPORTUNITY – IN 2080?   124
Speeding up the pace of change – equal representation, not just equal opportunity – objections to a programme for equal representation soon – qualifications and experience – 'women don't want more responsibility' – children – a core for the movement: institutions of learning – final reflections

NOTES and REFERENCES   139

SELECT BIBLIOGRAPHY   146

PREFACE

MY FIRST INTENTION was that this book should be strongly centred on the techniques being used, notably in the United States, to bring about equal employment opportunity between women and men, and on the part the women's movement had played, and continued to play, in securing the necessary legislation and stimulating the official agencies. This scheme for the book was closely related to my own pursuits, throughout the current decade, as an active member of the movement and as a student of equal employment opportunity policies. Part of the work I had carried out for the feminist organizations in which I held office was the creation of 'corporate plans' (borrowing a term from the business world): in these I attempted to look ahead for five or ten years, to specify objectives and to prescribe the change in financing and administration which would be needed to achieve those objectives. International Women's Year 1975 marked a watershed in the history of feminism: the principle of equality was accepted and intellectually respectable, and from then on implementation would be the major preoccupation. The establishment of International Women's Decade underlined that.

However, focussing on the interplay between feminism and the world of work (or paid employment, as I prefer to call it, for reasons which will appear later), I became aware of the difficulty of making connections between the approach adopted in the writings and attitudes of the contemporary women's movement and the extensive body of theory and practice which has been built up around the concept of work in the industrialized West. The historical women's movement won the vote, entry to the professions and many changes in the law affecting the status of women. In the 1960s, a new wave of feminism was founded on the realization that women were still at the bottom of the heap. Though they had flocked into the labour force, and the trades unions, they still earned less than men and were found in segregated areas of employment where their chances of rising to senior positions were negligible. Women might be full citizens in the legal sense, but economically they were very badly off – corralled into low paid employment and expected to do a second unpaid job in the home as housewives and mothers.

Yet the brilliant ideological attacks against what came to be called male chauvinism were mounted in other disciplines – literature, psychology, education, history, the arts. These were, of course, the subjects which women mostly pursue at school and university: even in our rebellion we are victims of conditioning. Despite the centrality of economics and of theories of business organization to the problems of women's inferior status, there was no feminist challenge to the economists, the organization theory experts and the high priests of the temple of management. Rousseau, Freud, D. H. Lawrence and even God were given no quarter by the women's liberation polemicists: but where were the feminist critiques of Ricardo, Pigou, Herzberg, Maslow and Drucker?

J. K. Galbraith has pointed out that women can go through a college course in economics without once realizing that members of their sex have a vital, unacknowledged and unenviable place in the production-consumption cycle. Women who have risen high in the business world, or even made significant contributions to management science, seem to have been subject to the same sort of blindness. Women have taken the theory and ideology of 'work' on men's terms, and sought to better their lot within that framework by agitating for legislation, banding together in trades unions or women's caucuses, or copying men's strategies for climbing up the hierarchy. Another school has embraced Marxism or revolutionary socialism, creeds which offer at least an analysis of women's unsatisfactory status under capitalism. Unfortunately, this brand of politics is so repugnant to 'capitalist' or social democratic governments that its theoretical contribution to the debate about 'women's work' is usually swept aside in a general rejection of its mainstream philosophy.

The ideological weakness of the women's movement in the socio-political, economic and industrial spheres is of particular importance at the present time. We are now seeing the establishment of more and more government agencies charged with the duty of promoting equal employment opportunity and overseeing the implementation of equal pay. These agencies cannot, by definition, adopt revolutionary tactics: they have to be 'acceptable' and to dress up their change-promotion activities in the garments of orthodoxy. If orthodoxy consists of a body of theory with heavy overtones of outdated patriarchy, the agencies will have an almost impossible task. What are personnel managers being taught in the courses leading to professional qualifications? What do executives learn at business schools? Do 'women's studies' feature in management courses? The answers to these questions give no encouragement to those who would like to encounter a receptive attitude to their equal opportunity programmes.

What we need is not more research into 'women's failure to achieve' in terms of the existing structures of organized work, but a thorough exposé of the sexism implicit in those structures and the theories which underpin them.

In this book, therefore, I have tried to contribute something towards a reappraisal of our ideas about 'work' in the light of contemporary feminism and of current attempts by governments to promote equal opportunity. I am neither an economist, a sociologist nor a political scientist. Only an amateur, no doubt, would dare to write a book offering a major challenge to these disciplines, not to mention anthropology and management science! My justification is that someone has to make a beginning. My qualifications include more than twenty years in paid employment of different kinds and a decade in the women's movement. What I have tried to do, in the true spirit of 'Ideas in Progress', is to point out possible directions for work by the people who are experts. Here and there I have suggested specific subjects for research which I believe would be useful.

I should also be glad if I were able to offer some basis, however rudimentary, for a feminist political and economic theory which starts from a woman-centred position rather than taking and adapting concepts from thought systems created by men without reference to women. It is difficult for women, as the dominated sex, to generate the self-confidence necessary for putting forward a woman-centred world view: but it must be done. Before we, women and men, can arrive at a truly human attitude, we need a fully articulated women's philosophy to stand up to (I believe that *is* the right phrase) men's philosophy. There is no short cut through the 'women's rights are part of human rights' fallacy.

Second, and for British readers in particular, I have felt it necessary to include some commentary on the women's movement, since it has been the subject of so much uninformed discussion, and so little impartial exposition. Sometimes observers from other countries express doubts as to whether there is a women's movement at all in Britain, and certainly it is very muted: some cross-cultural comparisons with other countries would be illuminating.

The third major component of the book derives from the original theme of the efforts being made to create and foster equal opportunity. Who are the change agents, and what chance have they of being effective? Are their objectives clear, and are they the correct ones to hold to? The choice between sticking to non-discrimination or adding affirmative action is one of the most momentous to be made in our age. Are we going to make it in a calm, rational and organized framework, in tune with our approach to scientific and technological problems, or shall we be overwhelmed by prejudice, the clash of interests and inadequate methodology?

4

One may well ask whether any conceptual framework can be big enough to accommodate an understanding of the millenial changes implied in the women's movement: changes which are fundamental to the physical, intellectual and spiritual life of one half of the human race and which continually impact on the philosophy, sytems and lifestyles evolved by, and depended on, by the other half? The answer must surely be 'No', if we are thinking in terms of an all-embracing theory or credo: but the attempt to find or create partial ideas systems is a natural and inevitable part of the movement. This book tries to reach toward such an ideas system in the sphere of work. At the same time, my thinking about work cannot but be influenced and enriched by parallel efforts in many other fields – art and culture, history, sexual relations, medicine, psychology, religion – the list could be extended almost indefinitely.

The thinking is new: but do the tools and techniques have to be forged specially too, as Jane Austen, according to Virginia Woolf, invented a new type of sentence; and as Emily Dickenson created her own verse form and punctuation? The phrase 'male-dominated' looms over the enterprise. How many of the techniques we use have been moulded in a one-sex pattern, not deliberately in most cases, but through the application of centuries of male bias? I remember how startled I was to hear a young Asian say from a public platform that science has been moulded entirely by Western needs and prejudices, implying that an Eastern science might be quite different. Can it be that such apparently neutral and objective techiques as logic, the scientific method and modern historical scholarship are not the reliable and impartial allies that we had supposed? If science can be dominated and vitiated by Western cultural norms, can reason and logic be suspect as male-dominated, perhaps even as instruments of oppression? Men have indeed never tired of telling women that they are not logical. Women have sometimes riposted that they could get to the nub of the matter quicker by using their intuition. How often have women listened to men conducting what *they* call a rational argument and have declined to take part because they perceive that what is being sought is not objective truth? Argument, logic are frequently a substitute for fisticuffs or other aggressive behaviour in man. Logic is a referee and whoever has more of it on his side wins the contest. Whether any worthwhile facts or principles have emerged is a secondary consideration, if it is a point to be heeded at all.

So while not denying that facts should be elicited and marshalled and that objectivity is desirable, one is aware of the limitations, even the obsolescence, of traditional forms of rational argument as aids to distinguishing fact from fancy and true propositions from fallacious ones. One should be willing to learn from the traditional, and often despised, women's approach to discussion and problem solving. While women were usually deprived of a formal education in the past, this does not invalidate the methods they used to deal with the problems raised by their own particular responsibilities, often in the ordering of human relationships. We know all too little about how the competent and successful wives, mothers, entrepreneuses, abbesses, political hostesses and salonieres of the past operated. All but a very few of them worked entirely through oral communication. Saint Teresa of Avila wrote her great devotional works somewhat grudgingly at the behest of higher authority. Like Socrates, she clearly felt that fact-to-face discussion and instruction were infinitely preferable to written discourses.

Enough at this point about male and female approaches to intellectual activity and problem solving. Meanwhile, in case any reader is made nervous by this questioning of reason, let me affirm that I believe in argument and debate in their proper place. I also believe that efforts to establish the truth by objective examination of the facts are always worthwhile if not always successful. Reasoned argument can be a true means of communication between men and women sometimes, and should be used when it is appropriate. Books have to rely on it rather heavily but it is easy to see why some of the world's greatest intellectual and spiritual explorers have thought it to be a rather impoverished form of communication.

ANATOMY OF A FEMINIST
A personal foreword

I DID NOT COMPREHEND sex discrimination until I was thirty-five. This is a measure of the way our society suppresses information and discussion on this subject. If one is fortunate enough to escape direct personal experience of discrimination, one can be unaware that it exists.[1] One cannot remain unaware of other social evils such as poverty, cruelty to children or racial discrimination. Betty Friedan in her seminal book *The Feminine Mystique* called the plight of the housewife 'the problem that has no name'. The status of women in general and discrimination against them is the problem which until recently has had no acknowledged existence. It was supposed to have been abolished in 1918–19. Now that it has been publicized through the activities of the women's movement, society has again shied away from the discomfort of recognizing it for what it is, by sub-dividing it into discrete special problems – 'battered wives', single-parent families, the lack of equal opportunity at work. The problem of sex discrimination is too burdensome, too overwhelming, and touches too many aspects of life: it is easier to reject the idea that society has an unhealthy and unjust attitude to the whole female sex. If any response is necessary, a liberal attitude to sex equality can be expressed; or a condemnation of the 'extravagances of women's lib' provides a convenient alibi for not engaging at all seriously with the subject. Despite the surfacing of sex equality as a newsworthy and discussable subject, it is still to many people a deeply embarrassing theme.

7

How was it that I managed to remain unaware of the real meaning, if not of the possibility, of sex discrimination? For the first ten years of life, I was an only child, until the family was completed by the birth of my sister. Until that time, I had been at co-educational schools, but for my secondary education I attended a convent girls' grammar school as a day pupil. Among the nuns and the lay teachers were women of scholarship and good judgement whom I admired and enjoyed learning from. Old girls who had gained university places or professional qualifications were held up to me as admirable models. Although we studied nineteenth century political history at advanced level, the syllabus included no mention whatever of the women's suffrage movement, and generally our education completely ignored the status of women and their contributions to civilization. The only distinguished women we were told about were the saints of the Church: as most of these were celibates, the study of their lives did nothing to awaken us to the problems of women in a heterosexual context. While my mother concerned herself with the question of whether I should marry and made it clear to me that I must try to look attractive (frowning was rebuked), my father was unswerving in his insistence that I should work hard at school, go to university and gain a professional qualification – marriage didn't enter into his scenario, it seemed. My teachers appeared to be of the same mind and it was while at school that I decided I would become a lawyer.

I was not particularly fired with enthusiasm for the law, but I passionately wanted to go to university where there would be greatly enhanced opportunities for learning: and I was already deeply convinced that economic independence was the most important goal in my life. To have to ask someone else for money for food, clothes, entertainments, travel, seemed to me an unbearable humiliation. I won a State Scholarship for my university course, but was deprived of all but a small honorarium because the grant was means-tested and my father's income exceeded the qualifying limit. Thus for another three years I had to live on my father's money when I had, in fact, earned the right to an independent student's income from the state.

The role models of my girlhood included my teachers and certain Catholic saints. Our nuns, of course, did not depend on men for money. They earned it by keeping a school. Clearly they were people of property – they owned a very large prime site in one of the best areas in the town, they invested in new school buildings, and they had really beautiful gardens which we could enjoy too. They went away for holidays every year (to a sister convent) and might be posted to houses on the Continent or, more adventurously, in Africa. They were thus cosmopolitan, and experienced travellers – they used to take parties of us to France in the holidays. On the whole, they were cheerful, intelligent and fun to be with – it was not unknown for them to join informal games of rounders, or even snowballing. They encouraged appreciation of music and the arts.

Other important role models were provided by two of my mother's cousins, one a senior civil servant and the other the Secretary of a hospital for women, where all the surgeons and doctors were women also. These ladies, both unmarried, used to come to stay with us occasionally and impressed me with their entertaining conversation and the breadth of their interests. They were both extremely good company and clearly led interesting lives founded on a responsible job which was quite well remunerated. It never occurred to me to ask why there was a hospital for women only. I suppose the convent school had accustomed me to the single sex organization, and even my co-educational primary schools had been run entirely by women.

Our kindly headmistress took seriously the task of preparing her older girls for life after leaving school. Most of us would get married, she said, but a few would have careers. The possibility of marriage *and* a career was not envisaged. In the conventual life, naturally, it was an impossibility – a career as a nun ruled out marriage. Did our headmistress assume that all other careers would be followed with such single-mindedness? No doubt, she did since the 'career

9

women' of the inter war period were usually single, like my two cousins, and it was hardly surprising that our head-mistress should not have foreseen the great surge of married women into paid employment – even the Ministry of Labour was surprised by this when it happened.

The idea that a career and marriage were incompatible was not one to dismay me. I had already in my teens assessed marriage as a poor option, which condemned one to financial dependence and domestic drudgery. Neither the experience of having a baby sister nor of looking after young children as an au pair girl in France one summer holidays produced in me any desire to have children myself. Children ceaselessly prevented you concentrating on anything and tired you out, in my experience. While certainly not disliking children, I realized that other people's could easily provide as much childish company as I felt I needed.

Those of us at school who had an eye on a career had our confidence built up. Sex discrimination was never mentioned. There was no doubt that intelligence and hard work was all that was required to succeed. (Just so, the President of Smith College, Massachussetts, the distinguished university for women, told me in 1975 that her students did not know what sex discrimination was until they entered the world of work). We competed against boys and girls alike in inter-school competitions in our town and did well in public speaking, Classical Association Latin speaking contests, and music and drama festivals.

At my university, young women formed about a tenth of the three hundred-strong body of law students. The women did well in the examinations. All but one of the teaching staff were men but we knew that there were some women in the profession. The textbooks told us how the legal disabilities of married women had been removed long ago. Single women had always been able to own and dispose of property. I interested myself in the history of English law and this had very little to say about the law's attitude to women, except in relation to the ownership of real property. I was not aware of the series of cases in the nineteenth century in which courts had ruled that a woman was not a 'person' in law, or of the way in which lawyers had resisted the entry of women into their own and other professions.

After the law degree, articles: and again I avoided any difficulties through joining a family firm. None of the women I knew had problems in obtaining articles and none of my women friends were heading for the Bar, so I did not hear about the difficulties women had in finding chambers which would accept them as pupils. When I qualified as a solicitor, I joined the Law Society and learned of the existence of the 1919 Club, a society of women solicitors.[2] I did not join it, since I could not see what possible function it could have – weren't lawyers lawyers, irrespective of sex?

From time to time, people asked me if I experienced any prejudice against women in the law, and I always replied 'No'. As a partner in a small family firm, with one major corporate client whose executives accepted me as fully competent to advise, I did not come up against anyone who disputed my right to practise my profession or cast doubts on my ability. I noticed that my women contemporaries tended to be employed in conveyancing departments but I avoided this by simply making it clear that I preferred the commercial and litigation work; I found conveyancing lacking in intellectual stimulus and it seldom led to interesting expeditions outside one's own office.

Even at a later stage in my career when I became the first woman to be appointed a departmental manager in a public corporation employing many thousands of people, the question of prejudice on grounds of sex seemed more or less academic to me. It was flattering to be interviewed by the house newspaper, and there was a feeling of achievement in being a 'first' in a very male-dominated industry.

At about this time, I attended my first feminist conference. It was advertised in *The Times* and I went along out of curiosity. I was sufficiently impressed to join the sponsoring organization, the Fawcett Society, but took no active part for two years. However, my early thirties were a crucial time of reappraisal in a number of ways. In this, I was typical of my generation of women executives.[3] Not only did I think seriously about my future at work, but I reviewed other aspects of life very critically. After fifteen years of 'dating', and a couple of what I felt were quite serious relationships, it became clear to me that the idea that I might one day get married was something which was created and sustained by relatives, friends and the social environment, and had nothing to do with any inner imperatives of mine.

My generation was the last before the 'permissive society' began. Marriage was the only possibility if one looked for a long term relationship. Marriage or, at the latest, the first child, spelt the end of paid work: there was a widespread belief that you could not satisfactorily combine a job and a family, which I shared at the time. The marriage option looked as bleak to me at thirty as it had at school. No man, however attractive, affectionate or intelligent, could compensate for the drawbacks of the married state from the woman's point of view – the financial dependence, the dreary mindlessness of housework. 'Mr Right' was a stupid myth; no one man could combine all the characteristics I thought desirable. Moreover, it seemed that men had little to give emotionally and tended to demand rather a lot. The idea of children was one which had no appeal either – the thought of being a mother was something totally shadowy. I fantasized about it but there was no reality for me. People told me that although children appeared to be noisy, dirty and disruptive, you felt different about them when they were your own: I had no desire to put this to the test. Nonetheless, I had marked time for a while waiting to see if marriage would come about. During my last affair of this period, I realized that I should have to make the proposal of marriage myself, if that was the conclusion I wanted. I decided not to do it. I would start structuring my career to fit my own preferences and ambitions and not some vague contingency of changed circumstances in an indefinite future.

Another reappraisal concerned religion. Brought up in a church-going family and educated in a convent, I had become an assiduous high church Anglican. The study of modern theology and biblical criticism led me to examine the Christian faith with a dispassionate eye. Gradually, I withdrew from all belief; even agnosticism seemed impossible. I still admired much in Christian ethics and religious practice and, above all, the belief that one must follow the truth wherever it leads, however distressing one may find this.[4] A major revelation was the close connection between theology and human male authority. Men had indeed made God in their own image and with no justification at all to my mind. Though I cannot now believe in any deity, the *idea* of God as a woman I find a great comfort and solace.[5]

Thus in my early thirties I had rejected, after a period of intellectual examination and appraisal of my own psychological make-up, some of the major assumptions about women's life and about religion which had influenced me as a young woman. I had determined to move out of law and into management, which seemed to offer more scope for the abilities I believed I had, and a career ladder leading to more responsible and, ultimately, influential posts. At thirty-two I had achieved the first step into management. I had also become aware of the existence of feminism. Perhaps it was inevitable sooner or later that some incident should precipitate me into full membership of the women's movement. This was in fact what occurred.

After about eight months in my second job of the adminstrative kind, in which I was the only woman among a small executive group, I was told without ceremony by my senior colleagues that it would not be possible for me to attend the Christmas lunch for the senior staff, or a lunch given for them by a principal client organization, because the first of these functions was traditionally held in an all-male professional club, and the second in an all-male senior executives' mess. For the first time in a career of fourteen years, I was faced with a categorical statement that qualifications and experience were irrelevant and sex was all that counted. I was extremely angry and made my feelings known. The insensitivity, the unfriendliness, and sheer petty-mindedness of this behaviour overwhelmed me. What was even more amazing was that I was apparently expected to accept it as something quite normal. Nothing could erase the memory of this insult and its underlying message – 'A colleague is not a real colleague if she's a woman'.[6] The following Christmas the wretched club relented: imagine my surprise at finding that all the waiting staff were women! Waitresses in the male sanctum of course underlined the subordinate status of women. (Some readers may think I make too much of this incident, which contributed to the motivation by which I became an active campaigner for women's rights. Substitute 'black man' for 'woman executive' and test whether this alters your view of the matter).

Even despite my awakening (or 'raised consciousness'), I was not at first convinced that equal opportunity legislation was a desirable thing. Like many women in professional or executive jobs, I did not want to be singled out as special or different from male colleagues. I was converted to the need for legislation by wiser and older women such as Nancy Seear and Joyce Butler, MP. I realized later that my ideal of being accepted as a 'brother' professional was naive. If anything further was needed, it was supplied by the senior management consultant who told me at an interview that I had all the qualifications and experience needed for a consultant in a particular division of his large company, but he would not hire me because I was a woman. Women, he blandly explained, were unacceptable to clients. I could have a backroom research job if I liked. I did not like.

My early furious anger at the contemptible behaviour of some men has abated in the eight years since I have been an activist, but it is necessary to explain the passionate feeling of injustice, and the attitudes towards both women and men which accompany it.

In another chapter, I evaluate the possibilities for men to be feminists or, at any rate, as some men have put it, 'women's liberation auxiliaries'. Men who have publicly aligned themselves with the feminist cause, or who have acted to improve the status of women in the face of inevitable opposition and denigration from other men, are comrades indeed, and their courage must be applauded. They are unfortunately few in number. More common are those who clearly feel that lip service to the significance of 'women's rights' is part of the kit of any liberal, socialist, marxist or proponent of alternative societies. These men are very unconvincing to female feminists, but even lip service has its propaganda value. Most suspect of all are the men who profess liberal and advanced views but whose vision of the future good society clearly rests on the continued subordination of women. A perfect example of this occurred some years ago, when a public lecture was given by an eminent industrialist on the theme that industry had to be organized to meet the aspirations of the people working in it. After an hour's harangue on the paramount importance of the people factor at work, questions were invited. I asked if the speaker would like to comment on the then government's proposal for a law giving equal employment opportunity to women. 'Oh dear,' he said, his face falling, 'I was afraid someone would ask that question', and went on to say that while some 'ladies' (sic) chose to work in offices, he was sure that most women preferred to be at home. So, for this advanced thinker, 'people' in industry plainly meant 'men' when it came to job enrichment and the humanizing of work routines and personnel policies. Another example of the invisibility of women workers. No one can respect a brand of liberalism which rests on assumptions about the continuing enforced supporting role of women. A skater who assumes that the ice on the pond will remain frozen for ever, or imagines that it owes him a duty to stay frozen, is a foolish fellow, however brilliant the figures he executes.

It is fashionable now to talk about the need for 'male' values to be balanced, or replaced, by 'female' values, if the world is not to topple towards total pollution and total war. Can men adopt 'female values' to a significant extent and thus control their own destructive tendencies? Perhaps, but if they do, I can readily envisage them rejecting actual women as only imperfectly embodying the 'feminine principle'. Alastair Mant in his book *The Rise and Fall of the British*

Manager writes of the housewifely, female element in management. 'The best production managers, like mothers, tend to have an almost feminine capacity to sense . . .' that trouble is about to erupt. However, Mant quickly reassures his readers that he is 'not suggesting a wholesale replacement of men by women in top manufacturing jobs. It wouldn't work.' (He does not explain why not.)

If men can be assumed on the whole to be inimical to women's liberation in practice if not always in theory, this is something to be expected; but it is bitter indeed for the feminist to bear the hostility and apathy of other women. It is clear that women have to take the initiative in improving their lot. If they do not will it, nothing can be achieved. The activist can be excused for feeling some chagrin at the way she is isolated by the sisters whose welfare she is fighting for, and at the failure of women's organizations to combine effectively. I remember a few years ago giving a talk on future directions for the women's movement to a branch of an organization for women graduates. The first question from the floor was 'Why don't you militants ever do anything for the housewives?' It is a curious logic which blames the housewife's, admittedly depressed, situation on the few women who are actively calling attention to the need to improve women's status. The true crime of the activists is to tear away the rationalizations by which women have been reconciled, or reconciled themselves, to the status quo.

The activist, then, can expect hostility from members of her own sex, hostility or cold-shouldering from men, and distortion and ridicule from the media. It is a hard task for a small number of women to combat all this and at the same time try to explain calmly what their true aims are. I am full of admiration for those who achieve this and remain balanced, and lovable, people, usually playing other demanding roles in the community in both paid and unpaid employment.

1 WOMEN'S WORK AND MEN'S WORK

Women's work

Women's work, the old saw runs, is never done. Modern research bears this out.[7] But what is 'women's work'? Is it as degrading and demeaning as some theorists and feminist polemicists suggest?[8]

First in the catalogue of women's work is the continuance of the human race by bearing children. In our own time, because of fears of over population, this function is sometimes seen as the exercise of a privilege, or even a form of self-indulgence: but in all past ages keeping up and increasing the stock of human beings has been of prime importance. The expectation of life was low and child mortality high. The obloquy and shame traditionally heaped on the barren woman illustrate the high value which was placed on women's reproductive role. When every kind of work was labour intensive, the demand for 'hands' was never-ending. Children were the only form of insurance for old age. Even today the belief lingers that national prosperity is linked with population increase, so that the falling birth rates in Europe are taken as a bad omen, despite countervailing anxieties about world population growth and high unemployment.

Next, woman's work is to feed the people she has brought into being. In modern industrialized countries, we have largely forgotten woman's role as a cultivator, but world wide more women are agriculturalists than are in all other occupations put together. We say, in our Biblical tradition, that 'Adam delve' and 'Adam was a gardener' but in reality Eve has been the cultivator and food provider and in many

17

countries of the world she still is. Even in industrialized countries where agriculture has been mechanized, women predominate in the food processing and preparation industries and in catering, restaurants and hotels.

Third, it has been woman's work to clothe people. Spinning and weaving have been her province, and the making of garments. The notion of clothes bought ready made in shops is a very recent one, and before that only the wealthy were able to afford the services of a professional tailor or dressmaker. Textile production also included household linens, wall hangings, bed covers and other requisites. These traditional functions have carried over into the industrialized state, where great numbers of women are engaged in textile production, garment making, and retailing of clothes, domestic textiles, and haberdashery.

Fourth, women have tended the weak and frail members of the race – small children, the sick, women in pregnancy and childbirth, the elderly and the disabled. When these functions are institutionalized, women continue to perform them as nurses, midwives, medical ancillary workers, childminders, social workers and voluntary workers.

Fifth, women have been responsible for the education and nurture of young children of both sexes, and of older girls. Women today form the majority of the teaching profession, and in the past the job of governess was one of the few paid occupations which upper class women could undertake and remain 'respectable'. Many women's religious orders undertake teaching.

Sixth, women have taken charge of the house, home or shelter. Sometimes they have constructed it themselves. They make it warm, comfortable and attractive. They furnish the textiles, implements and pottery needed by the home economy. They keep the dwelling place clean. Within living memory, women formed a great labour force in domestic service and in our own time they still do this work either as freelance workers or as employees of cleaning companies, or unpaid as housewives.

Such is and has been the work of women throughout the

ages. All these functions, which I call 'the six tasks', pre-date the money economy, and all of them arise from a bedrock of necessity – these things cannot be left undone if the human race is to survive and life is to be tolerable. Women could in the past feel pride in their work – the self-deprecating confession, 'I'm only a housewife', is a modern phenomenon. As Olive Schreiner said in her description of the immemorial role of women as workers 'We knew that we upbore our world on our shoulders; and that through the labour of our hands it was sustained and strengthened – and we were contented'[9].

The effect of the industrial revolution and the development of modern technology and the welfare state has been to make immense inroads on the integrated concept of woman's work as the sustainer of the world. Specialization and the division of labour have at last been applied to woman's work – centuries after they were commonplace in man's work. Everything that used to be made at home from soap to sugar lumps, from cough remedies to candles is now provided by mass production. Children go to playgroups or to school at a early age. Old people live in 'homes' or geriatric wards, the sick are looked after in hospitals and convalescent homes. There are still mothers who take care of their disabled children at home, daughters who tend ageing parents, but on the whole such care is the business of salaried professionals. The institutionalization of childbirth and the deathbed has also much diminished women's position as stewardesses of the mysteries of birth and death. This does not mean that women are experiencing the emergence of leisure. More and more take up paid employment and combine this with the vestiges of the old roles. What is left to us to do we try to perform to an ever higher standard. We worry more than ever our grandmothers did, I suspect, about discharging our responsibilities as parents and feel guilt rather than shame if a child of ours goes astray. Food may be bought already prepared, but we strive to create great variety in the menus.

Another facet of women's work which has, I believe, developed significantly and almost unnoticed, is that of emotional shock absorber and confidante. Wives have traditionally played the role of confidante to husbands, and mothers to children. However, they did not have to bear this role alone. The priest, the doctor, the school teacher and members of an extended family were all available for 'confidential counselling', as we should call it now. Today few resort to the churches; the doctors and schoolteachers usually have too many people on their hands to give adequate time to individuals, and the extended family is a shadow of its former self.

It is no longer acceptable for the stresses of the workplace to be worked off in drunkenness, street fighting or violent pastimes such as the old kind of football (virtually a free-ranging fight) and bloody sports involving animals, like cock-fighting and bear-baiting. Violence towards other members of the family is regarded as an aberration and a social evil. In our time, work and living conditions are greatly improved, compared with the historic conditions of the mass of poor manual labourers. Nonetheless, other tensions arising from the increased discipline required in most forms of work, and from the massing together of millions in conurbations, now make themselves felt. The threats to the physical and mental health of people (predominantly men) in positions of high responsibility in business and all kinds of administration are well documented. The rat race precludes the use of fellow rats as confidantes and advisers – the atmosphere is far too competitive.

The effect of these trends is that more and more problems, moods and strains have to be expressed in and worked out through the family, centering on the wife and mother. A woman who has been trained in dealing with psychological problems may manage these difficulties successfully, though still at a cost to her own inner resources and peace of mind. Most women have to sink or swim, doing the best they can, often not really understanding what is happening and becoming frightened and tense themselves.

An increasing number of men desire their wives to be receivers of the psychological waste products of the day's work. It is possible that one of the unacknowledged reasons why some men still do not like their wives to take up paid employment at a demanding and responsible level is that they fear the wife's mind will no longer be a blank page on which to scrawl the diary of their day's events because she will have her own burden of problems and frustrations which she wishes to share. The difficulty is that a woman who has experienced nothing comparable to her husband's work is not going to make a satisfactory counsellor. This may be one explanation of the affairs between managers and secretaries: a secretary knows so much of the business, she does not have to be given long explanations of the current situation or of the personalities and actions of colleagues or others who are causing difficulties for her manager. Nor is she competing for his job, so she can safely be made privy to his anxieties.

Thus, whether or not the wife feels that she can cope with the roles of confidante and emotional buffer, those roles are a growing responsibility and impose strains upon her. They may also create a feeling of personal inadequacy.

Though the majority of women work longer hours than men, there is a minority who have free time, usually because their husbands' income is ample and their children have gone into full-time education or left home. This leisure is often used for voluntary social service and charitable work, either through organizations, or freelance in the sense of performing services for old or sick neighbours or relatives or work on community projects of all kinds. These unpaid services are 'work'. They clearly relate to women's traditional preoccupations of caring for the weak and disadvantaged members of their society.

It would be inappropriate to leave the question of women's work without a mention of religion. Women have been high achievers in the Christian faith which is, or was, the religion of the countries of the industrialized West. They have been outside the power structure of the priestly hierarchy but that has made no difference. Women have been saints, miracle workers, theologians, writers of great devotional works, founders of religious orders and, indeed, of whole sects. Men did not feel that their interests lay in down-grading or hushing up the religious achievement of women – quite the reverse. Thus many a woman has been beatified or proclaimed a saint by the Roman church and benefited from the hagiographical efforts of fellow believers: whereas achievements of a comparable level among women in other spheres have been neglected by historians and popularizers alike.

For many centuries women who professed as nuns escaped the dangers of childbearing and probably led an altogether healthier and pleasanter life than their sisters in 'the world'. The cloister gave women the opportunity to exercise authority, to rule over great estates, to practise the arts and to enjoy dignity and esteem as useful members of the community and occupants of a recognized place in the great corporation that was the Church. In our own times secularism is the norm, and celibacy is almost an unmentionable topic. Nonetheless I am sure there is something to gain from the study of women who lived such distinctive lives as abbesses, hermits and mystics. They represent notable feminine achievements. What were the conditions which fostered such achievements? Are there lessons to be learned here for the secular worlds of business and industry?

What do we mean by 'work'

The review of 'women's work' which we have just made attempts to trace some of the history behind the rigid segregation of the labour market in industrialized countries. When 'new work' has been created, it too has been sex-classified. Thus women's paid employment has expanded through the opening of new areas of work – for example, those involving office machines, from the telephone and typewriter up to the present day computer, and in the production of electrical and electronic goods. We need to find out more about what causes a particular type of work to be classed as 'men's' or 'women's' and why the sex classification of the same type of work differs from place to place. This research would help to illuminate the reasons for 'women's work' being almost always low in prestige and in pay.

In this section, however, and before going on to examine the idea of 'men's work', I should like to look at our concept of 'work'. When we speak of 'women going out to work', or ask a woman 'Do you work?', we always mean paid employment: but as we have seen, a great deal of 'women's work' is unpaid. The six tasks all pre-date the money economy. All of them are capable of being done for monetary reward, and many of them are nowadays, but there is still an enormous amount of work in the six tasks category which is done, unremunerated, at home, or voluntarily outside the home.

It seems, therefore, that our idea of 'work' is one of those concepts which has some sex-bias built into it. For men, 'work' is indeed paid employment, and activities outside the job are hobbies or sports. We cannot make this neat division in the case of women.

The Concise Oxford Dictionary defines work as 'expenditure of energy; striving, application of effort to some purpose'. This seems to me open to the objection that it also applies to activities which could be categorized as 'leisure'. A man who spends his spare time making model boats for his own amusement is 'applying effort to some purpose', but we do not call his activity 'work'. A woman expends a tremendous amount of energy during childbirth, but we do not call this 'work'. However, unlike model boat building, it is certainly not 'leisure'.

The consequences of this principle that 'work' is the same as 'paid employment' are extremely important. The principle affects a person's right to an old age pension, to social security benefits and to help in disablement. It affects one's social standing. It makes a difference to the availability of training relevant to one's 'work'. In modern industrialized countries, it has been associated with great stress on the importance of 'productive work', that is, paid work in factories and mills where most goods are manufactured. Engels, who was much concerned with the unsatisfactory status of women in the last

23

century, felt that it was absolutely necessary to get women out of the unproductive drudgery of the home and to give them a share in productive work: only then would their lot improve. Where one's standing in the community and life chances appear to depend utterly on how much money one possesses or can earn, the logic of this view is compelling. Feminists have justly insisted on women's 'right to work'. However, it would be useful now to put some thought into why unpaid work has such low prestige, and whether we can find ways of enhancing its status. This is of importance not only in relation to the position of women in society, but also, in an era of declining job opportunities and ever-shortening working hours, and years, to men, who tend to have far more emotional capital invested in 'work' and to become mentally distressed when it is not available. (There was even an instance recently of a man's suicide being attributed to redundancy, when the steel mill in which he worked was closed down and no alternative employment was available.)

The definition of 'work' I should like to propose would be one covering all activities which contribute to the continuance of the human race and to the welfare of human beings, whether remunerated or not. Work is that which must be done if the human race is to survive, or which, if it is done, makes for improved living conditions or a greater sense of well-being. Work is directed first to survival and thereafter to making life more secure, comfortable and agreeable. Work may be physical, intellectual or emotional. The concept of emotional expression or effort as work is quite alien, of course, to the conventional idea of work. The more specialized and organized 'work' becomes, the less place there is in it for the emotions. This again, I believe, is the effect of male bias. Men prefer to distance themselves from the emotional aspects of life. If human behaviour can be conveniently docketed in accordance with a system, they feel happier. The personnel department and the welfare officer are there to cope with emotional messes. Not for nothing has personnel been assigned a 'female' role among the functions of management.

The adoption of such a definition of 'work' as I have just outlined has important repercussions on the definition of 'leisure'. The Concise Oxford Dictionary offers a definition which looks harmless enough: 'free time, time at one's own disposal'. In the next section, I shall look at 'men's work' and commit the heresy of suggesting that a great deal of what men claim to be 'work' is in fact far more akin to leisure.

Men's work

There is an impression that men do most of the world's work. I have suggested that on the contrary women have traditionally done the essential tasks within the definition of 'work' which I have adopted, and that they continue to do many of them.

First let us examine men's share in the six tasks. Then we will look at other forms of 'men's work', traditional and modern.

The work of populating the world is of course shared by men in that sexual intercourse is essential to conception. However, man's part is easy and brief compared with woman's which involves the inconveniences and pain of menstruation, pregnancy, miscarriages, lactation, greater susceptibility to venereal infections, and the continuing perception of vulnerability associated with these conditions and events, which is heightened by the fact that, alone among the mammals, the human female has no 'closed season' for intercourse.

Man's part in food production is thought to stem from the earliest era of humanity, when hunting is said to have been the major or unique source of food. Much emphasis has been placed on 'man the hunter' and I think a good deal of fantasizing has gone on. It is often assumed that women took no part in hunting at all. This seems to me very much open to question. It cannot be assumed that when humans lived in primitive tribal groups there were no women capable of stalking and killing animals and birds, catching fish, or collecting small shellfish, grubs and other meat. It is rather more credible that fewer women than men might engage in hunts involving the tracking of large savage animals over long periods and killing them at close quarters with primitive weapons. However, women are capable of throwing spears and shooting arrows. In any case, humans can survive without animal food. Meat preparation, from the killing of animals through the processes of butchery and dressing of joints tends to be a male occupation, though women have usually undertaken the entire business of raising, killing and dressing domestic poultry. Sea fishing is a male occupation but the processing and selling of fish is often handled by women.

Thus men have been associated with food production involving prolonged absence from the tribal settlement (hunting and deep sea fishing), and lifting heavy weights (whole carcasses or large joints, nets full of fish). In agriculture they became involved when deep ploughing was initiated and demanded considerable physical strength. As populations increased, agriculture became a business and more men were engaged in it. The selling of surplus agricultural produce was one of the foundations of trade. Trade involved long absences from the settlement – witness the drovers' tracks which cross the country. Drovers could be weeks on the road, taking herds to market.

Men's part in textile production and making of garments has also been linked to the ability to travel. The wool in medieval Europe was based on the collection of produce (either raw wool or finished goods) from numerous small production units and its transport to centres for further processing and sale. Thus while the producers were women (and men) of humble status, the merchants were men.

The fourth area of women's work that we listed was tending the weak and frail, including babies and small children. Here men are not to the fore. Monks operated some hospitals in the medieval period, but most sick and elderly people have been cared for at home, and attendance on pregnant women was the province of wisewomen or midwives. The male midwife appeared late on the scene and was eventually outlawed in Britain under the Midwives Act 1902 .[10] The custody of the insane in institutions was undertaken by men, but the treatment of inmates was brutal until twentieth century advances and cannot be classed with the devoted care of the home nurse. Professional nursing was the creation of Florence Nightingale and her followers. Scientific medicine is a modern phenomenon and like other male-dominated professions is associated with high prestige and high profits and an instrumental and technical, rather than empathetic, approach.

Other 'social work' which has been undertaken by men in the past includes the functions of jailor, executioner, workhouse master, governor of foundling hospital and petty judicial functionary. In these capacities men certainly had to deal with the vulnerable and downtrodden but the image they have left behind is one of hard-faced discipline, cruelty and corruption, rather than of care and understanding. The most famous pioneer of prison reform in England was a woman, Elizabeth Fry. People of all classes would make the most strenuous efforts and sacrifices to keep members of their families out of institutions.[11]

In education, men have had charge of older boys, either as schoolmasters or private tutors. Higher education has been exclusively in the hands of men, and men have been its exclusive beneficiaries, with a few exceptions among royalty and members of the leisured classes. Only in the last century was any move made to enable women to study to university degree level.

Finally, the provision of shelter: when this takes the form of permanent buildings made of material which has to be hewed and dressed, men seem to take over completely as builders. Architecture has been practised by men alone until the present century, but its great monuments are not homes, but civil and ecclesiastical prestige projects and town planning on a grand scale, sometimes combined with speculative building. Men have, however, contributed greatly to utility, comfort and elegance in designing and making furniture of all kinds, glass, china and cutlery and innumerable useful

of wood and metal. Originally created for the pros-
these comforts are now available to all. Glass in
s, damp courses, water closets, improved kitchen and
equipment, central heating, have all added to the
convenience of dwellings and made 'women's work' in running the home easier. Indeed, as we have already noted, they
have contributed to making the traditional housewife redundant. The capital intensive home is a male creation.

We see, then, that men share, and have shared, in varying
degrees, in the six basic types of work needed to sustain and
continue the human race. Their part has been influenced by
their possession of greater physical strength, and they have
benefited from profitable opportunities for specialization and
commerce, from which women have been excluded. Women
cook, men become chefs; women make clothes, men set up
as tailors and couturiers; women tend the sick, men practice
medicine professionally.

Our image of 'men's work' today is not drawn from the
six tasks, however. 'Men's work' is, and has been, sharply
contrasted with 'women's work'. While a high proportion of
men were, before the industrial and agricultural revolutions,
engaged in agriculture and animal husbandry, and the peasantry of both sexes was the substratum on which all higher
orders of society rested, the division of labour and exploitation of slave and near-slave peoples had long before resulted
in surplus manpower which could be employed in activities
concerned with affairs beyond the basic necessities of life.
There were people who, through their control of the labour
of others and of materials, found themselves relieved of the
need to do any work at all. Leisure among the leaders of
society required occupations to fill their time and engage
their talents. The occupations which were created, or elabo-
ated from more primitive forms, to supply this need were
fourfold – warfare, religion, law and government, and learning and the arts. All these activities called for leaders and for
followers or practitioners, and all of them provided ways of
using materials surplus to basic needs. At worst they could
usurp resources which were needed for survival, as when

armies on the march stripped the countryside of all supplies of food.

Whatever the origins of war among primitive peoples and whatever its significance in evolutionary terms (if it has any) it became a way of life in Europe. From the end of the Roman Empire in the fifth century AD to the fall of Napoleon (and perhaps beyond) war was the pride and recreation of privileged males, the career of the mercenary and the intermittent occupation of the poor man. The whole structure of medieval society revolved around the need to raise armed levies, and numerous crafts ministered to the warlike art. When war was not actually in progress, tournaments, hunting and 'manly sports' provided mimic versions of it. Foreign conquest, in the name of religion or trade, provided alternatives to civil war and local conflicts within Europe. War was not thought of as a woman's occupation, a fact still reflected in the laws of heraldry: women entitled to a coat of arms may not display it on the usual shield shape but only on a diamond shape known as a lozenge. Women campfollowers ministered to the domestic needs of armies but they were classed among the lowest levels of society. For men, war was noble and honourable, but any woman who might appear qualified to share the glory was denigrated as a freak or a whore. Joan of Arc was condemned as a witch.

War and its sporting substitutes cannot qualify as 'work'. Far from enhancing life, war made it hideous for the peasantry and small townsfolk, and hunting took its toll in ruined crops; game laws reserved animals of the chase exclusively for the ruling class, severe penalties being visited on poachers.

Religion, on the other hand, in its primitive forms, shared with work the characteristic of being necessary (in the perceptions of people at the time) to survival and well-being. Human fertility was a major preoccupation of religion, which was also invoked to prosper agriculture. In medieval Europe, religion evolved into a power structure and partook of the nature of leisure – it became concerned with inessentials, in the end to such a scandalous extent that the Reformation and

Counter-reformation were required to purge it. The Church took over the primitive rites and festivals and transformed them into more 'spiritual' occasions. Its institutions became rigidly hierarchical and extremely rich. It became involved in government, was a major landowner, dominated all scholarly and artistic activity and supplied virtually all 'white collar' workers, since reading and writing were not considered an essential part of the education of the warrior aristocracy. It also involved itself with war and was the initiator of the Crusades.

Unlike war, religion was not an exclusively male occupation, but priesthood, and therefore entry to the hierarchy, was. Great abbesses could be both powerful and learned. Like superiors in the male religious orders, they held sway over dozens, perhaps hundreds of people – members of the order, lay sisters, employees or tenants of the convent's lands. However, these great ladies may be seen as an extension of the territorial aristocracy rather than an integral part of the religious power structure. There was no way in which they could enter the priestly caste or aspire to the higher ecclesiastical orders and dignities. (Veneration of women as saints occurred officially only after the death of the subject, sometimes many years, even centuries, after.)

It may seem perverse to exclude government and law from the category of 'work'. Surely they are universal features of human society and indispensable to communal life at whatever degree of civilization? As with religion, one may distinguish between the primitive and sophisticated forms. Every tribe and society has customs and rules, and when a society becomes too large for a general assembly of its members to make all necessary decisions about group activities, there is delegation to a person, or group of persons, who exercise the necessary authority. Similarly, the settlement of disputes is displaced from the simple folkmoot to a specialized forum where cases are pleaded by professionals. Only a society with spare resources can afford professional lawyers and bureaucrats, and from time immemorial they have been distrusted and stigmatized as parasites and oppressors.

The development of the arts and scholarship, like the elaboration of law and theology, can also be seen as a function of leisure. Patronage for the arts came from the church and from monarchs, aristocrats and rich merchants. These also endowed places of learning, which were originally staffed by clerics who were, by definition, male. When the grip of the Church was loosened and secularization set in, artists still depended on the patronage of the wealthy. Places of learning were more independent since they could count on a continuing flow of fees and endowments and had already, like monasteries, accumulated revenue-producing assets. Science began as the hobby of wealthy amateurs.

In modern industrialized societies, relatively few men are involved in the traditional occupations of agriculture, production of hand-crafted goods for domestic use, war, or ecclesiastical employment. Only a few will take part in government or the administration of the law, or in the artistic or scholarly professions. The majority are employed in the winning of raw materials and fuels; in manufacturing and engineering; and in the many types of scientific, administrative, financial and managerial work which modern industry calls for. Transport and communications also employ many men. Some 'men's work' still requires prolonged absence from home; some still involves heavy physical work or very unpleasant working conditions, but this is less and less the case as technology advances. Much of what men do comes within the definition of 'work' that I have adopted, but some of it still looks like a lineal descendant of the old leisure pursuits. Before investigating this line of inquiry, however, we have to go back to 'women's work' and see how it has evolved.

'Women workers' and 'ladies of leisure'

In the long ages before the step change introduced by the industrial revolution, the mass of the people, of both sexes, was engaged in basic survival and a subsistence level economy. Insofar as the production of surpluses enabled activities to be carried on over and above the subsistence level, these were conducted almost exclusively by men. The money economy meant very little to most people who lived on the land and whose few trading activities were still not far removed from a barter system. Personal savings were virtually unknown and the banking system, which emerged during the late middle ages, served the needs of governments, and of merchants who traded internationally.

The absence of women from such remunerative and prestigious activities as government, leadership in war, ecclesiastical office, high scholarship, the judiciary and international trading can be explained in part by the demands (and casualties) of childbearing and childrearing, the employment of women in the other five tasks of basic survival, and the consequent difficulty for most women of engaging in any activity requiring prolonged absences from home.[12] Wives in the mercantile and artisan sections of the community however shared the responsibilities of the family enterprise and benefited from its prosperity.

With the mechanization of production, and of agriculture, and the introduction of improved husbandry, the home ceased to be the workplace. Manufacture by machine required large specialized buildings and many 'hands', since the work was machine-aided, not automated. Men, women and children flocked into these mills and workshops. Population increased by leaps and bounds. The 'proletariat' had come upon the stage of history, accompanied by full scale 'capitalism'. Another, apparently inescapable, feature of the new economy was the trade cycle – boom was followed more or less regularly by bust, with consequent effects on the demand for labour and the level of wages. The urban masses, unlike their peasant forebears, could not eek a minimal living in hard times, and the only social security came through the workers' own self help organizations. Thus, to be 'in work' was almost literally a matter of life and death. Trade unionism was undeveloped and subject to severe legal restraints. Competition for jobs was intense. Food was no longer produced by oneself and one's neighbours. It came from shop keepers, street vendors and, in Britain, ready

32

cooked from the fish and chip shop. Milk was sold at the door from a churn.

Woman ceased to be the food provider, the bread maker, and man the bread-*winner* emerged. At the same period, conditions of work were so arduous and unpleasant (and often unhealthy) that it became a goal for women to avoid work in the factories altogether. Men wanted wages large enough to enable them to maintain their wives and families without the need for the wives to go 'out to work'. A wife who stayed at home was also a status symbol, indicating the husband's high earning capacity. She was on a par with the middle class ladies whose function was to demonstrate, by elaborate idleness and lavish entertaining, their husbands' success in business. Reformers reinforced this trend by securing legislation which limited women's capacity to do paid work – forbidding them to work at night, or in certain kinds of job, or more than so many hours at a stretch. However, these efforts to reduce women's participation in the labour market were not entirely altruistic. Men did not want women competing for jobs, particularly as their lower rates of pay threatened male wage rates. Women were debarred from joining trade unions in most industries in Britain. Trade unionism among women was a weak plant, and many women were employed in circumstances which made organization extremely difficult. Securing equal pay for women was recognized as a solution to the undercutting of men's position in the labour market by women, but was not pursued with any enthusiasm by the male trade unionists. The employers had their own reasons for opposing it. Women were a useful cheap source of labour which could be sucked in and dismissed to fit the employer's response to the state of trade.

Working class women had obstacles in their way, but women of the upper classes found it impossible to work at all in the occupations pursued by men of their own social standing. Matrimonial property law prevented married women going into any trading activity on their own account. Women's entry into the professions was bitterly opposed, and access to any form of higher education was made as difficult for them as possible. The notion of their participation in government as voters or legislators was also rejected, although men were being progressively enfranchised.

Summing up, we can say that for most of recorded history in Europe, the majority of the people lived on the land. Insofar as there were opportunities to follow occupations other than agricultural ones, they arose out of trade and commerce or from the ability of people who obtained command over resources and labour to leave work to be done by others. These opportunities were available only to men. Women continued to follow a much older pattern of existence, based on the six tasks, and there was little specialization or division of labour in 'women's work'. When agriculture ceased to predominate and urban industrial life got under way, women became dependent on the power of men to earn money. Women were employed in industry to some extent, but both for humanitarian reasons and in order to eliminate competition, women were excluded from full participation in paid employment and from allied activities, such as trade unions, vocational training and higher education. Such paid work as women did was closely allied to the traditional six tasks, whereas the range of occupations open to men was increased spectacularly by industrialization and the expansion of trade which accompanied it.

The effect of the agricultural and industrial revolutions, of colonization and the opening up to the West of what are now called the developing countries, has been to increase leisure, so that all sections of the population in industrial countries now take part in it. The former distinction between necessities on the one hand and luxuries or leisure goods and activities on the other, has become blurred. Survival is assured, and interest focuses on the standard of living and the quality of life. It is a commonplace of economics that we depend to a great extent on the production and sale of goods and services which people would not want unless advertising suggested such a need to them. In this sense luxuries have become an economic necessity. What counts today is job security. 'Work' is no longer the individual's contribution to basic survival, well-being and continuance of the community – work is what you do to obtain a regular income. 'Leisure' is what you are engaged in when not 'working'. Activities which fall under the definition of work which I have adopted but which are not remunerated exist in an uneasy limbo. It is simpler to ignore them, and economists have done so, as we shall see.

'Work' is a system made by men for men

Paid work takes a wide variety of forms, as any national list classifying people's occupations will show. However, with few exceptions (such as clergy, artists, some self-employed people and outworkers employed by manufacturers) paid work is no longer a home-based activity. Mass production, and the building up of large organizations, require employed people to come to a work centre – factory, office, transport depot and so on. Some older forms of paid work, such as mining and maritime occupations, were by their very nature carried on outside the home. We have already observed that 'women's work' was home-based because childbearing and rearing made it difficult for women to take up occupations at a distance from the home. Paid employment in modern times is the descendant of earlier forms of industrialized, mass-production employment and is based on male requirements and lifestyle. Insofar as women were obliged to conform in the earlier days of factory work to these male norms the results were felt to be a cause for concern.[13] 'Protective legislation' was enacted to curtail the working hours of women (and children) and to forbid their employment in certain kinds of work. It was not suggested that there was much wrong with the system as far as men were concerned, and such defects as there were could be ameliorated through the power of bargaining with the employer and by trade union pressure.

Let us look at the features of organized paid work today which stamp it as a male-oriented system. Hours of work demand attendance at the work place for eight or nine hours at a stretch with only short breaks for refreshment. Overtime, or managerial responsibilities, frequently add further hours to the same shift. Shift work proper is becoming more common and many people work at night. The corollary of this insistence on work being done in eight-hour slabs is that part-time work, which many women seek, is regarded as a second best.

Continuity of work is also regarded as a virtue. The ideal employee is one who wins the gold watch for thirty or forty years of service to one organization. Better still, he will have missed very few days on account of sickness. Holidays are typically taken in slabs of one or two weeks, often at the same time, so that a whole plant will shut down for the holiday fortnight.

Women will, more often than not, break their working life for a period of childrearing, returning to work on a part-time basis at first, perhaps. They require time off to care for sick children and other relatives and for discharging many other family responsibilities. Younger women want to use employment as a means of 'seeing the world'. Large businesses have been built up on the basis of supplying women's demand for temporary work and short-term jobs. Women want their jobs to fit them. Men will accept that they have to fit the job, and therefore there is no point, and some disadvantage, in men's shopping around the labour market. Men who have a long list of previous employers are suspect – they will be unstable 'drifters'. Among men's jobs, those taken by itinerant workers have low status – building site labourers, motorway gangers, scrap-yard workers, for example.

In men's work, at all levels, there is an emphasis on staying put in a job. There are also rewards in the form of seniority systems, incremental pay scales, long service increments, promotion ladders, pension schemes and other fringe benefits. Insofar as women tend to have broken career patterns, they miss the opportunity to collect these rewards, or they benefit from them less than men.

A requirement of some executive and professional work is

mobility, either in the sense of being free to travel on business for short periods, or in the sense of being willing to move around the country, or abroad, for longer tours of duty. This presupposes that the employee has no dependants whom he cannot leave to look after themselves for days, or even weeks, at a time, and that in the event of a posting to a new location his dependants can and will uproot themselves to follow his star. The use of the pronoun 'he' is apt here, as married women will encounter difficulties and resistance if they travel on business leaving their husbands and children, or if they suggest that their husbands should give up their jobs and spend a spell supporting their wives' careers in a new location, perhaps finding themselves a temporary job locally. Such an arrangement is still thought to be unnatural by most people.

Work is organized hierarchically and still, largely, in authoritarian modes which most women find stuffy and distasteful. There is a great deal of management by oration, and lengthy meetings at which much talk occurs but little to the point. Women's mode of operation tends to be informal and direct. They have quick perception and quick reaction. It is not being argued here that their approach is either superior or inferior – but it is different, and the corporate bureaucracy is not a way of life in which women feel at ease.

Yet another feature of the employment structure which works against women (and is open to criticism on other counts, too) is the split which is so often enforced between advancement in career terms and practising the art and skills which attracted one to one's chosen occupation to start with. This is particularly true of the skilled occupations where women predominate: 'success' in teaching takes one further and further away from the classroom; 'success' in nursing means moving into the administrative hierarchy; 'success' in social work involves increasing detachment from the details of case work.[14] The same phenomenon can be observed in many other places, however, and can affect men also. Men seem more willing to sacrifice job satisfaction to ambition, but for many women, the majority I would guess, the rewards

37

of promotion – authority, power, pay and fringe benefits – do not outweigh the deprivation expected from leaving behind the opportunity for creating and appreciating at first hand the end product of the system – children achieving their potential, people being helped through illness or distress, and other direct contributions to human welfare and development.

This obsession with hierarchy and its accompanying bureaucracy is seldom, if ever, questioned. Why is administration more valuable than the work which is being administered? Why can we not reward people for doing the essential task, instead of forcing them to abandon it if they want or need to earn more?

The demand for a career ladder is closely allied with the male worker's life pattern. Men want, or are conditioned to expect, that they will 'get somewhere' in the course of their working lives. Julia Davies (op. cit. p. 34) notes that in 1970/71 male nurses, though a small minority in the profession, held 33% of the top nursing officer posts in England and Wales. Do men reluctantly accept the need to depersonalize their work if they are to advance in status and pay, or do they regard the basic tasks as just a means to an end and sigh with relief when they can leave them behind? Is society making a wise choice in rewarding people for distancing themselves from the work which directly determines the level of welfare in all kinds of situations?

Unlike other animals, humans have found ways of producing and storing large surpluses of food; thus they do not have to spend the major part of their time and energy on the daily or hourly search for food. The free time or leisure thus created has benefited men far more than women, who have been absorbed in the six tasks to the exclusion of other activities.

With leisure comes boredom, an underrated but highly influential factor in human history. Numerous devices and pastimes have been invented to fill up leisure time – hunting, sports, board games, cards, gambling, elaborate meals, drinking, theatricals. Games are more exciting if something is at risk. The most exciting game of all is war, an all-male game. Not only is life at risk, the supreme gamble, but the whole organization of war and the conduct of campaigns provide numerous exciting diversions – the designing of uniforms and accoutrements, military reviews and manoeuvres, treks over strange country, sleeping in tents, the camaraderie of the mess, the fun of planning strategy, looting and rape, the glory of victory, a man's 'honour' to be cherished and enhanced, the risk of losing honour if one fights badly. Neither the loss of life nor the devastation of the countryside and crops could be set against the compulsive thrill of going to war. If there were no hostilities in progress, men had to make do with hunting and warlike sports to alleviate the aching tedium of a rural existence.

It is difficult to believe that the instincts which led to continual armed conflict for centuries have died out completely though, thanks to nuclear weapons, they have not much chance of expression along traditional lines as between 'advanced' countries. Old fashioned warfare is now practised only in developing countries. Is it too fanciful to see the business world as the modern substitute for the old time theatre of war? Here a man can command a platoon, a battalion, a regiment or even a whole army. The enemies are commercial rivals, or other divisions of the same organization, or 'the managenent' or 'militant workers'. The executive dining room is the officers' mess, the board meeting is the council of war, there are scouts and spies. Science and technology are recruited to provide ever improved 'weapons' (new products or more efficient processes). Life, either in the sense of one's job, or literally in the case of potential victims of executive stress, is at risk. Those who lead the victorious troops sit among the great ones of the land. There is widely-available loot in the form of fringe benefits, expense accounts and employee discounts on company goods. Sexual harassment of female employees is condoned and envied. 'Leadership' – the key quality in war – is highly extolled in business, too.

Anyone who has worked in a large organization knows that far more goes on inside it than is strictly related to producing and selling the goods or services whose provision is the ostensible and sole reason for the existence of the organization. A great deal of work is extremely boring, and the mind turns to other aspects of life in the organization. Even people who are seen patronizingly as working 'only for the money' have a great involvement in what goes on at the workplace. Ambitious men see the production and sale of the product as a means to their personal ends. Executive life leaves plenty of time for scheming, intriguing and games playing. Organizations provide excellent resources and intrastructure for carrying on these ploys – comfortable offices, secretaries to type memos, telephones, canteens and dining rooms for meeting people and lobbying. 'Office politics' is an inadequate description of this web of endless activity.

Organized paid work offers numerous opportunities for individual conflict and mock warfare. Men will form a loyalty to their organization which can result in a 'my company right or wrong' attitude in dealings with others. The great expansion of multinational companies offers a colonization experience in place of the real thing, which disappeared with the end of imperialism. Competition with other companies can also take on the form of war, with forays on potential markets, propaganda and (industrial) espionage. Companies can play cops and robbers with government agencies which are charged with monitoring or controlling facets of business activity. This theme in the world of work is elaborated in Anthony Jay's books *Corporation Man* and *Management and Machiavelli*. Jay puts forward the premise that life in the organization, whether public or private sector, is a substitute for the primitive brotherhood and aggressive instincts of 'man the hunter' and of medieval 'bad barons'.

In modern industrialized countries, children are banned from the workplace. Laws forbid their employment, and company policy and custom decree that they may not be brought on to the premises. Few organizations make any provision for employees' children such as crèches.[15] In this aspect also therefore 'work' is structured to fit the male life-style, the corollary being that women are at a disadvantage. (Another side effect is that the great majority of children grow up with very little idea of what 'work' is about, never having experienced life in a workplace.) The absence of children, pregnant women and young mothers reinforces the maleness of workplaces and the ethic of hardness and sternness. Gentler emotions, and deep feeling generally, are taboo at work. An exception is anger which, if not welcome, is not regarded as inappropriate as a response to circumstances arising at work. Anger is a warlike emotion. Women however are not supposed to show anger or any form of aggressive behaviour. Women at managerial level are doubly deterred from showing natural emotion by the fear that by doing so they will prove the 'truth' of the criticism that women are emotional and therefore unfit for responsibility. Emotional behaviour will undermine their own positions and also make life more difficult for other women seeking to climb the corporate ladder.

Stendhal (quite a feminist in his way) says in his book *De l'Amour* that women have to spend their lives listening to men talking about things that are supposed to be important. Paid work has its importance, but that is not the same thing as saying that all paid work is important. The superstructures of self-aggrandisement, empire-building, industrial conflict, and the sheer wanton waste or misuse of resources cannot all be respectably cloaked by the dignity of the appellation 'work'. Men play their games, while women stand by and watch, unable to influence what is going on.

Women's contribution – actual and potential

During a seminar at the Massachusetts Institute of Technology in 1964,[16] a speaker made the point that scientific work was always the same, regardless of the sex of the person doing it. Feminists have striven to establish that most, if not all, kinds of paid employment today share this characteristic (though long-established custom has led people to divide

41

work into 'men's' and 'women's') and, furthermore, that the ability to perform any particular kind of work satisfactorily is not likely to be found predominantly among members of one sex rather than of another.

It is not incompatible with such a viewpoint to accept that, at present, it may be the case that women have a different attitude from men to the organization of work, and to the manner or style of performing it. This difference may also embrace the question of priorities between paid work, unpaid work and activities freely chosen in the life of the individual.

There is a dangerously thin line here between the uncritical adoption of stereotypes, and a genuine, but unarticulated, perception of a difference between the sexes. Some people, myself included, find that, while they have dismissed the crude stereotypes, they can still half believe that there are attitudes, or bundles of attitudes, towards employment and the way work is done, which are more likely to be held by members of one sex. While one would not assume, in an actual situation, that any particular individual held these attitudes, one might in general discussion say 'A woman would have handled that problem differently', or 'Can you imagine a group of men discussing the issue from that angle?' In arguing the merits of an organization composed of both men and women, as opposed to one staffed predominantly by members of one sex only, these generalized perceptions about attitudes may perhaps be of some use. This will be so, however, only if we can agree that they have some kind of validity and that the attitudes in question will be held consistently irrespective of the milieu in which the people are working. To begin with, it would be useful to have some descriptive and comparative studies of employing organizations which are all-male, all-female and mixed. Are there differences in the way such organizations go about their business? If so, what are they and how do we account for them? Do the differences bear any relation to stereotypes, or to the kind of vague assumptions about gender-based behaviour which I have just described? Are these differences attributable to education, social conditioning or individual circumstances?

As we shall see later, in the literature on women in employment there is much emphasis on women's ability to perform to male standards and expectations. What is lacking is any systematic examination of the contribution women may have to make as women in the world of paid employment.

To clear away one fallacious line of thought, I should state that I am not thinking here of the stereotyped classification of woman as being specially suited for certain work because they are 'good at dealing with people' or because they know about being consumers, are 'conscientious about detail', or can 'represent the woman's point of view'. It is arguable that all these approaches are a form of sex-discrimination rather than a genuine attempt to employ women's particular capabilities ('Well, if we've *got* to have women in here, let's keep them in traditional female roles'). I remember that after I had secured my place on the London Business School Executive Programme (which I had favoured because of its emphasis on numerate skills), I had a long argument with an official in the Ministry administering grants, since he wanted me to abandon the London opportunity and take a course in personnel management in Sheffield; and when I first asked about openings in management, personnel was suggested, by the Personnel Department, as the obvious choice.

It may be objected that to maintain that women have a distinctive contribution to make is contrary to feminist principles. However, for the foreseeable future, I think such a proposition can be entertained without compromising the feminist position on equal opportunity. In the ideal, non-sexist world of the future, it will be recognized that human abilities are not sex-linked. It has already been shown that there is more similarity than difference between the sexes, and this will be generally accepted. Job specifications and selection tests will be prepared according to methods which are not gender-biased. For the purposes of employment, the guiding principle will be that a person is a human being first and a woman or man a long way second, if this is relevant at all.

Today we are very far away from this ideal situation. The world of paid employment is saturated with the results of gender-conditioning. Sex stereotypes abound. The culture of business is a male-dominated culture. At the operative level, sex determines the kind of work you can do: at managerial levels and in professional and specialist jobs, sex determines how high you can go and what you will be paid. Volumes of statistics bear witness to this. Some women have managed to transcend these limitations, but only very few. They are exceptional, not in terms of innate ability, but of lifestyle. They have arranged their lives so that they avoid the limitations which hold other women back. This is very clearly brought out by the case studies of 'women who made it' in Hennig and Jardim's study *The Managerial Woman*. A prime strategy is not to marry or, if married, not to have children. Women with children may employ others to take care of them, or work from home using paid domestic help. A woman who owns her own business will be more free to take time off when it is convenient than one who is employed in an organization. (Varieties of these arrangements are described in the Rapoports' book *Dual Career Families*.)

Even the women who, like myself, opted for the single, childless life, would vigorously resist the charge that they are 'imitation men'. Yet it has to be admitted, while dismissing the derogatory stereotypes of 'hard' career women, that it has been difficult for a woman executive to resist adopting the corporate lifestyle which is, of course, masculine. (The alternative is to feel oneself perpetually at odds with the way things are done.) The result of this conformity is, unfortunately, that the women involved may come to feel that other women who have not joined in the struggle are just feeble and could achieve much more if they made an effort. The woman who has been a high achiever in business is thus liable to feel that there genuinely is no difference between high-flying women and their men counterparts. Such women have both rationalized away the differences and overcome a good deal of their gender conditioning. In this sense they are 'ahead' of most women. As they have been produced by exceptional circumstances and exceptional personal effort, we cannot expect that they will become numerous.

Whatever the distinctive contribution of women may be, it is in my view very unlikely to be realized until the isolation of women in executive positions comes to an end. This isolation exists not only because of the extremely small number of such women but because of the way they are viewed and treated by male peers. In the past, women have also tended to dislike being seen to seek out the company and alliance of female peers, if there were any, as they felt this would accentuate their separateness as 'women managers'. However, this attitude is now beginning to break down, as women realize the value of exchanging information and know-how, of mutual support, and of solidarity in approaches to management on issues affecting women.

No-one's contribution to any form of endeavour is likely to be released fully and effectively when that person feels she is not really one of the team, is constantly under scrutiny and always having to prove herself. For these reasons, it is necessary for women to be seen in quite large numbers in non-traditional roles in the organization. Not only will this break down the isolation deriving from numerical scarcity but it will accustom men, and women, employees to the idea that a woman in an executive position is a human being like other human beings. In this atmosphere the women will relax and be able to develop creative and spontaneous approaches to work instead of looking over their shoulders all the time. Other women in shop floor or junior white collar jobs may be encouraged to break out of their low level positions.

The proposition, which I put forward later, that women managers should form the same proportion to men managers as exists in the workforce generally (about 40%) takes us into an entirely novel situation. The increase in women managers will have to come (as the increase in women operatives has come) through the employment of married women, including those with children of school or pre-school age.[17] Such a development also opens up the possibility of a substantial number of part-time managerial posts. If they are available for women, they will have to be made available to men, too. We may be surprised at the number of men who take advantage of this. The introduction of the part-time manager will have an interesting, perhaps dramatic, effect on the whole, slightly mystical, concept of what a manager is in the Anglo-Saxon countries.

The distinctive contribution of women, then, can be looked at in three ways: the effect, first, on personnel policies and, second, on concepts of management of the entry of substantial numbers of women into the mangerial grades; and third, the effect on organizational culture of women no longer being a tiny minority in such grades and therefore free to express themselves rather than to conform. In their book, Hennig and Jardim describe how, after twenty years or so of submerging their personalities in the corporation culture, the 'women who made it' felt that having achieved success they could at last relax and express themselves with some spontaneity. They adopted a personal style which expressed their individuality instead of the anonymity of a corporate hack who knew it was important to play down absolutely the fact that she was a woman. When women cease to be a minority in management and can combine managerial careers quite licitly with 'being their own woman', their contribution and creativity on the job will burgeon.

With blue collar women, the problem is not that of numbers, for they are well represented at shop floor level. The interesting speculation is what will happen when they become significant as members of the skilled worker elite, and spread into a much wider range of occupations. Shop floor power for women, not just in trade union activities but in worker participation and decision-sharing, is an exciting concept.

One of women's major contributions is that their centre of gravity is not in paid employment, and they can (unlike any men of whom this is true) be open about this fact, as society approves women's involvement in home and community. Even unattached women will usually go for a balanced mix of paid employment and outside interests rather than put all their eggs in the career basket. The reverse attitude, prevalent among men, makes them extremely vulnerable: when they are unemployed or made redundant they suffer acutely and have nothing to fall back on. Typically, the female attitude is described negatively as lack of ambition or drive, lack of 'loyalty' to the organization, instead of positively as exhibiting a sense of proportion, of balance between intellect and feeling, external achievement and interior development.

It would be salutary if equal opportunity agencies put some work into interpreting in such positive terms other characteristics which are supposed to make women unfit for the higher corporate life, or even employment of any kind. Absenteeism is a good example. Absenteeism in fact demostrates how *responsible* women are (not the reverse) since it is often caused by the illness of their children or other domestic problems of this kind. A comparative study of the activities of women and men on days of absenteeism might be illuminating.

A great deal of effort has been invested in showing that the disadvantages of employing women are not as great as they seem. It is time that the women's movement had the confidence to claim that there are advantages which are far more important; and that the so-called negatives are not as negative as they are made out to be. Womanpower is being wasted by societies which hypocritically bemoan the dearth of managerial talent and skilled 'manpower' but continue to proclaim that educating and training women for industry is wasted expenditure.

Much, if not all, of the research on 'women in industry' and 'women at the top' seems to me to be beside the point and the results not helpful in dealing with the major problems of establishing equal opportunity which is just as important for blue collar women. It seems sometimes that there is an obsessive search for an answer to the question 'Why do so few women reach senior positions?' carried out in a conceptual framework which by its very nature makes it impossible for a 'solution' to be found. The fact is that 'the system' makes it impossible for women to 'achieve' in the system's own terms.[18] To question 'the system' itself is not in contemplation but since women's 'under-achievement' is perceived as a blot in societies which claim to offer equal chances of advancement to all their citizens, the futile quest for an 'answer' to this problem has to continue.

Instead of conducting more research into women's alleged 'failure to achieve', attention should be directed to women's successes, and the lessons that can be drawn from them. Case studies based on businesses created by women could usefully be introduced in management training curricula at business schools and similar educational establishments. The distinctive contribution of women in building up a number of today's professions should be investigated. One can instance nursing, social work, housing management and, particularly relevant to the theme of paid employment, personnel work.

Personnel work, historically, was an area where women made a major contribution in Britain. In fact, they could be said to have invented the profession, which grew from the activities of women factory inspectors around the turn of the century and started out as 'industrial welfare work'. Welfare was widely interpreted, and included such matters as the engagement of staff and the regulation of piecework systems as well as the improvement of working conditions, though the tasks were seen as mainly lying among women and young people. (The companies which pioneered the concept were principally large employers of female labour.) The work was tough and had to be carried out in the face of suspicion from managers, supervisors and trade unionists. The founder members in 1913 of what is now the Institute of Personnel Management comprised twenty-nine women and five men. From the beginning, practitioners operated in a professional manner: there was no question of voluntary charitable effort. Mary Wood, the first industrial welfare officer to be appointed (by Rowntrees of York) and the Institute's first President, was a major innovator in business practice, backed by an enlightened management who gave her a free hand.

By 1927, the Institute had 420 practising members of whom fewer than twenty were men.[19] In 1929, Nora Wynne became the first welfare supervisor to join the board of the employing company, when she was made a director of Carrs of Carlisle.[20] It was not until after the Second World War that personnel management began to be thought of as a career for men too. It was extremely popular with men returning from war service and by 1950 half the Institute's members consisted of members who had joined since the war; at the same time, women represented slightly under half of the members as against three quarters in 1939, and this swing towards male membership continued in subsequent years. As Mary Niven puts it[21] 'Not only had personnel management become recognised and established, *it had somehow also become respectable with the wish of men to make it their career*.' (Stress added.) In their evidence to the House of Lords Select Committee on the Anti-Discrimination (No. 2) Bill,[22] the Institute quoted a study made in 1970 which showed that the women were concentrated in the more junior personnel posts; and the survey sample included ninety Directors of Personnel, not one of whom was female. By 1972, women comprised only 19% of Institute membership.

Here then is a remarkable case study (which could probably be paralleled in the development of social work as a profession) of an area of major industrial significance pioneered by women. The end of the story – acquisition of virtually the whole field of senior positions by men – especially raises questions of interest and merits detailed research.

Can we conclude that women are used as pioneers and risk takers by industrial society but somehow conditioned not to seek or demand the fruits of their endeavours?

When personnel work began to cover employees of both sexes, why was it assumed that men could deal with women but not women with men? Mary Niven herself suggested that it was because management was thought of as a male function that men began to dominate when the scope of personnel work was further widened in the post-war years. However, her own narrative shows that women industrial welfare workers were seen from the beginning as 'representatives of the directors' as Seebohm Rowntree said. Perhaps a crucial factor was the inclusion in the personnel remit of pay negotiations with the trades unions. Still today 'indus-

49

trial relations', that is, the area of conflict between management and employees, is seen as a male function within personnel. The industrial welfare movement was dedicated to reducing the sources of conflict by humanizing working conditions, promoting training and providing efficient channels of communication. Has the new personnel profession a vested interest in strife? Have men taken over 'female values' (and rejected actual women), or have they perverted them? Would women just spoil the war games of industrial relations? I urge the study of women's and men's part in the evolution of personnel work.

Women have also made some outstanding contributions to management science.[23] Mary Parker Follett (1863–1933), Lillian Gilbreth (1878–1972) and Joan Woodward (1916–71) are among the best known, but they certainly do not stand alone; and there are a number of women practitioners today doing distinguished work. What is not clear is whether one can identify aspects of their work which could be characterized as distinctively feminine. If there are such aspects, what is their nature – choice of research topics, early awareness of usefulness of new techniques, emphasis on the worker as a person, all-round rather than narrowly specialist approach, presentation of results?

Another interesting feature of the work of such women, at least in the past, is that they appear to have accepted without question the subordinate and unsatisfactory position of women in industry. Thus, in a volume of the collected work of Gilbreth and her husband, Frank (who died in 1924), there is only one indexed reference to 'women in industry, attitude toward' which leads into a passage in the chapter 'Motion study for the handicapped'![24] Addressing the seminar at the Massachusetts Institute of Technology on 'Women and the Scientific Professions', Gilbreth managed to say nothing at all on the subject of the seminar; her remarks on women were confined to emphasizing their role as homemakers turning out happy and co-operative employees for business. However, she was in her mid-eighties at the time, so this speech may not be typical of her views. Gilbreth herself had suffered humiliatingly from sex-discrimination in a number of ways, despite her recognized high place in her profession.

Both Gilbreth and Follett had great breadth of vision and they lived through the era of the suffrage campaign and other feminist endeavours. It is, therefore, impossible that they can have failed to appreciate the issues: did they ignore them and, if so, in what spirit? or have their views on women's position in industry simply been ignored by male editors and writers on management science? Another interesting avenue for research work.

Management style is often cited as an area where women have something special to give, particularly in connection with the movement from paternalistic to participative systems. It is said that they are accessible, sympathetic, informal, unstuffy, direct in getting to the point, not prone to stand on their dignity, realistic, concerned to get the best from people for the latter's own benefit as well as for the organization's sake, spontaneous, honest, averse to wrangling, ready to 'grasp nettles' in human relations, brief in discussion. Of course, it is possible to think of examples of women who are not like this and of men who are. The worthwhile thing however, would be to lift this dimension beyond the level of the women's magazine personality test or amusing dinner party topic and explore it systematically. Consistently with my general approach, I would advocate that any research on these lines cover men as well as women: if men indeed tend to be long-winded, pompous and formal, we want to know to what extent and why.

It seems obvious that one reason why women might be inclined to get to the point quickly and not waste words is that they have more to pack into the day than men: there simply is no time to waste. Men managers will extend the working day into the evening, knowing that when they get home there will be food, drink and warmth waiting. Women will long before that want to be away, seeing to the children's supper, doing some late shopping, preparing for husband's return, just ensuring that some family living takes place in the home as distinct from its being a mere depot for feeding, watering and sleep. As a single person without dependants, I have joined in these evening sessions for many years and I am extremely sceptical about their usefulness, especially since I have seen so much of normal working hours wasted in garrulous meetings, unnecessary fussing over detail and failure to delegate. Spinning out the working day encourages an undisciplined approach to work. One may be forgiven for suspecting that a prime objective is to avoid sharing household tasks.

2 THEORY AND IDEOLOGY

'With quiet indignation I broke in.
"You misconceive the question like a man,
Who sees a woman as the complement
Of his sex merely. You forget too much
That every creature, female as the male,
Stands single in responsible act and thought,
As also in birth and death" '

Elizabeth Barrett Browning
Aurora Leigh   1856

The explosion of industrial and trading activity in the last
two hundred years was matched by an expansion and development of intellectual and political activity. Attempts
were made to explain and predict the confusing phenomena
of the trade cycle; and the perceived shortcomings of
industrial society stimulated efforts, both scholarly and
passionately political, to map out a better world and devise
better and more human methods of organizing mass production.

We are still living with the results of these endeavours
today. Since women were originally, and continue to be, very
under-represented in these fields, theory and political dogma
have been evolved from a male perspective and have done
little to improve the situation of women. There have been no
woman-centred intellectual systems; where the concerns of
women have been recognized at all, it has been in a piece-
meal or incidental fashion.

Politics

The founding fathers of American Independence repudiated the idea that the Rights of Man should be extended to women, although women had played a significant part in the revolution of 1776. Nor did the leaders of the French Revolution of 1789 accord political rights to women. However, the nineteenth century saw the emergence of systems of political thought which acknowledged the position of women to be a problem worthy of serious consideration. Treatment of the 'oppression of women' is a common feature of Marxist, Communist and Socialist theory and is there linked to the institution of private property, which requires women to be monogamous so that a man may be sure that his children are indeed his, and that his material substance will not be inherited by another man's progeny.

Best known in this field is the work of Marx and Engels. Their analysis of the evils of capitalism probed into the structure of the patriarchal family to which they ascribed the subordination of women. They saw the privatization of women in the family and their exclusion from productive work as a major form and, indeed, the primary form of oppression of human being by human being. Hence the emphasis in communist theory on freeing women from 'slavery' in the family and enabling them to work outside it. If these views seem exaggerated, it must be remembered that they were evolved at a time when in law a married woman had no right to any money or property of her own, no right to the custody of her children. Husbands could beat, or lock up, wives with the sanction of the law and confiscate their earnings. There was no divorce, and even when it was introduced, adultery by husbands was condoned, while adultery by wives was classed as a matrimonial offence. It is, therefore, not hard to see why Engels said that, in marriage, the husband was the bourgeois and the wife the proletariat.[25]

What might be called the feminist dimension of socialist and communist politics has been well explored in Juliet Mitchell's *Woman's Estate* and Sheila Rowbotham's *Women, Resistance and Revolution*. There are two points to note here.

First, as Mitchell observes (p. 76ff.), no progress has been made from these early formulations towards specific political programmes designed to achieve the emancipation of women from the drudgery of unpaid work in the home, and their liberation in the form of equal participation in paid productive work. Second, the male members of egalitarian political groupings in practice can behave just like sexist oppressors themselves.[26]

Conservative or right wing political theory can be as sexist as the behaviour of left wing or minority group political activists. In extreme forms it is concerned with 'keeping women in their place'. In societies which are heavily dependent on women in the paid labour force, and where women have political rights, conservative parties are obliged to have a policy on the status of women. This is likely to focus on equality of opportunity, by which is meant the removal of legal constraints. Women should not be debarred from any job, or from appropriate training, just because they are women. However, conservatives stop short of willing the means by which women can be enabled effectively to compete in the male-oriented world of paid employment. Emphasis on the family will mean that provision of child care facilities by the state is ideologically distasteful. On the other hand, there may be a willingness to alter taxation laws in order to accommodate the two-career family. Conservatives are more likely to include the well-off members of society in their ranks than other parties, and the wife who has no paid employment is a feature of conservative political circles. Conservative women are expected to spend time giving voluntary support to the party and to raise funds for it. Thus they are very unlikely to be a source of pressure for improvement of the status of employed women, and will tend to see women executives as rivals for their husbands' jobs rather than 'sisters'. The slogan 'Make policy, not coffee!' is unlikely to appeal to them.

A couple of years ago, I was invited to the United States Embassy in London to meet a woman who had successfully stood for election to her State Legislature. Asked how she picked which party ticket to run on, she said she had chosen the party through which she was most likely to get elected. One can only applaud this pragmatic recognition that no party's ideology or practice has much to do with issues of interest to women. Why should they, when politics has been created by men to deal with issues of sharing or not sharing power and wealth among themselves? The choice is to use existing party structures as best one can, or to form a Feminist Party, as in France, to quote one example. It may also be that emergence of 'single issue politics' in the United States has something to do with increased poltical activity by women, who have one of the world's lowest levels of female representation in the legislature.

A number of studies have been made of women's voting patterns and the suggestion has been made that women tend to be conservative. What would be interesting is a study of the 'barriers to entry' which keep women's political participation so low, and an analysis of how and to what extent political activity has in fact contributed to improvement in the position of women. How can the barriers be lowered? How, meanwhile, can women obtain the results they want from the male-dominated political system?

Economics

In our own time politics have become overshadowed by economics in Western industrialized countries. It was in these countries that economics was created as an indentifiable discipline, and they still produce many of its leading exponents. Classical economics came into being through attempts to understand the complex relationships involved in industrialized societies. Increased prosperity was offset by periods of slump and considerable distress among workers as work opportunities contracted drastically.

Economics took its root in theorizing about demand and supply and the associated price mechanisms, including wages. It was wholly a creature of the money economy and strove to be scientific, that is, to discover natural laws governing the economic activity of human beings. Any operation which could not be expressed in terms of money prices fell outside its scope.

We have noted already that the six tasks of women all predated the money economy and that many of them are still performed for no economic reward. Thus, economists' measures of 'work', such as gross national product, leave out of account these unremunerated activities, which are vital to society and its well-being. In view of the domination of politics by economics, it is difficult to overestimate the importance of this large gap in economic theory. As J. K. Galbraith has succinctly put it, 'What is not counted is often not noticed'.[27]

While the muted participation of women in political life has enabled political theorists and activists to ignore them, the massive increase in the number of women, particularly married women, taking paid employment since the Second World War, together with the stimulus provided by the new women's movement, has prompted economists to examine women's activities and the economics of the family. They have also considered the economics of labour market discrimination, both on grounds of sex and race, and of equal pay policies. We have as yet no 'economic woman' to place alongside the economist's long cherished 'economic man', but at least a beginning has been made.

Before looking at some of this up-to-date thinking, I should like to illustrate the treatment of women in economics by reference to the work of a notable writer who stands midway between the classicists and the modern era, a distinguished contemporary of Keynes, and the holder of the Chair of Political Economy at Cambridge. A. C. Pigou (1877–1959) pioneered a new concept in his book *The Economics of Welfare* published in 1920 and still today regarded as a major contribution to economic thought. He diverged from the classical economists in that he thought 'the main motive of economic study is to help social improvement' rather than provide a description of inexorable economic laws. He also diverged from the classical doctrine stemming from Adam Smith that if every man pursued his own interest intelligently, with the minimum outside regulation, the results would be conducive to the benefit of society as a whole. Pigou saw that there might be a distinction between profit to the individual and profit to the community. He used the idea of the 'national dividend', meaning not spendable income but all the goods and services produced by the country's capital equipment. Policies and practices are judged in his work on the criterion whether they tend to increase or diminish the national dividend. An increase in the national dividend is assumed to increase general economic welfare: as there are few rich people and many poor people, the poor are likely to benefit generally from any increase in the national dividend (Part II, Chapter VII). (Pigou speaks of society as being composed of 'the rich' and 'the poor' which no doubt reflected the conditions of the early twentieth century when he was writing.)

Pigou recognizes the deficiencies of economics in relation to 'women's work' and invented the famous economic joke, 'If a man marries his housekeeper . . . the national dividend is diminished' (p. 33). He says that if protective legislation obliges women to move out of paid work into unpaid work at home, 'the national dividend, *on our definition*, suffers a loss against which there is to be set no compensating gain'. (Stress added.) Nonetheless, he cannot bring himself to throw away the measuring rod of money.

Pigou denounces artificial restrictions on access to jobs, on the ground that maldistribution of labour is liable to injure the national dividend, and he points to 'traditions and customs' prohibiting women from undertaking certain occupations as the most important of these inhibiting factors, in Europe at least (pp. 507–8).

He also appears sympathetic to what might be considered a feminist point of view when he proposes that a prohibition on factory work for women immediately before and after the birth of a child should be matched by provision of financial relief for families who cannot afford to lose the woman's wages.

However, when it comes to other practical matters, in his

examination of wages, Pigou offers no comfort to the woman worker. He recognizes that there is such a thing as an 'unfair wage' which he defines in a technical sense, as related to the marginal net product, and includes among his examples the very low pay of home workers, many of whom are women tied by domestic duties: but he says that any outside action to force up their pay would be detrimental to the national dividend, because their marginal net product is low compared with factory production which is mechanical. I find it difficult to follow his argument (p. 554, note 2) but he seems to be saying that because they are by definition home-bound they cannot improve the distribution of labour (and therefore the national dividend) by taking a factory job. There is, therefore, no justification for paying them more for staying where they are. Turning to exploitation (that is, payment of wages less than the value of the marginal net product), he says that interference to increase the wage is justified (but not practicable in the case of home workers), mainly because it is a kind of subsidy to inefficient employers who, if wages were fair, would be obliged to improve their equipment and methods. However, Pigou acknowledges that his analysis does not explain the difference between men's wages and women's wages, and he proceeds to examine what he calls this 'special problem' (p. 564ff.).

Proposition one is that there is no unfairness in the fact that women's day wages (i.e. time rates) are not equal to men's, because women's 'natural endowments of mind and muscle' are not, on average, equal to men's. However, if piece rates are unequal between men and women, this does require explanation. The explanation given is tortuous. It emerges that, in theory, in the very small number of occupations where men and women are equally efficient, piece rates should be equal, with the proviso that men should have an extra allowance because 'they can be put on night work and can be sworn at more comfortably' so it is 'more convenient' to employ them. In practice, however, there may be situations where piece rates are unequal, but equal pay for work of equal value, or even for work of greater efficiency by women, is not justified, because employers will then give up any attempt to establish women's right to do this type of work in the face of the customs and traditions to the contrary. Women's great advantage is that they are cheaper labour and this 'advantage' must be maintained in the interests of breaking down sex monopoly of work, enabling women to enter jobs at which they are more efficient than men, and thus increasing the national dividend.

New economic theory is grappling with some of the problems that Pigou recognized. The approaches range from iconoclastic to highly mathematical. J. K. Galbraith in *Economics and the Public Purpose* focuses on the essential role of household consumption in the modern advanced economy, and the search for alternatives to the personal services formerly supplied by domestic servants. The neoclassical economic concept of the household, in his view, has served to disguise the fact that women have been transformed into a 'crypto-servant class' organizing ever more elaborate consumption and servicing the family. The more prosperous the family, the more burdensome this work becomes, so that among the wealthy, the wife is debarred from any outside activities except voluntary work which will not impinge on her main preoccupations. Being a good housewife is a 'convenient social virtue' calling forth praise from the more powerful members of society who benefit from it. Social disapproval follows on the neglect of domestic duties. Galbraith sees the male monopoly of better jobs as the result of the perception by the 'technostructure', that is, the men who control businesses, that if women do not continue to facilitate ever-increasing consumption the economy will be in serious trouble. Galbraith's prescriptions follow the lines of United States policies of equal opportunities both in employment and education. He advocates provision of professional care for children and greater individual choice in the structuring of the work week and the work year. He posits that there will be a shift of the economy into services as women's consumption-organizing work diminishes. (This shift seems to be observable already.)

The Civil Rights movement and the women's movement have led to much economic analysis of discrimination. Nobel prizewinner, Paul A. Samuelson, who uses a mathematical approach, proves that the removal of discrimination increases gross national product. (Translated into Pigou's terms, this seems to imply that the loss occasioned by discrimination to those discriminated against, is greater than the gain discrimination brings in the national dividend.) Samuelson qualifies his statement by pointing out that the withholding of training from women means that as yet women are not always equally efficient and therefore not completely interchangeable with men as his economic model requires. Findings from both macro- and micro-studies of employment tend to support a feminist point of view. Analyses of pay show invariably that there is an inequality between men and women which can only be put down to discrimination, other factors such as educational attainment, length of service and so on having been allowed for in the comparisons. (It could be maintained, of course, that some of the factors eliminated to arrive at residual discriminatory inequality are themselves features of discrimination in the education system and in personnel practice.) In a British study of sex differentials in teachers' pay, it was suggested that one reason for the lower pay of married women was their lack of mobility owing to their husbands' employment; thus the area in which they looked for a post was circumscribed.[28] However, writing in 1975, Dr Andrew I. Kohen[29] commented that economists still had not evolved a theory capable of explaining the phenomena of unequal pay. Nor had they uncovered the mechanisms by which discriminatory attitudes are given expression. A related point is made by Chiplin and Sloane[30] when they draw attention to the need for more study of hiring practices. Sex is used by employers as a 'cheap screen', that is, a way of deciding between applicants for a job which involves no management time or effort.

The most researched aspect of women's employment is the reasons for their levels of participation in the labour force. 'Economic man' has been seen as making a choice between paid work and leisure: not whether to enter the labour market at all, but how much paid work to do, whether to work overtime and so on. To explain the more complex phenomenon of women's choice, economists use the concept of the cost of time, and recognize that women can divide their time in three ways – paid work, unpaid work in the home, and leisure. The research has been extended to fertility – the choices as to the number of children and the spacing of their births – since this clearly has an influence on women's economic activity.

Economics has therefore travelled some way towards recognition of 'economic woman' who is no longer hidden completely within the family unit. A considerable body of academic literature is devoted to this field, and it is encouraging that, in the United States at least, a number of women economists are practising in this area of study. Unfortunately, much of the work tends to be somewhat recondite, involving statistical techniques and showers of fearsome looking algebraic equations. One becomes a little sceptical about the need for all this science when one is offered as a tentative explanation of series of statistics the conclusion that 'child care uses a woman's time much more intensively than a man's'.[31] Even Pigou, who is not much addicted to algebra, breaks out into a rash of equations in his attempt to explain the difference between men's pay and women's pay.[32] Is this a characteristic male retreat into abstraction when faced with a knotty problem in human relations? I hope that a modern Harriet Martineau will be inspired to write a book on the economics of sex discrimination which will give us the fruits of the valuable and interesting work that is being done, but in terms which people who are neither statisticians nor mathematical economists can understand. Meanwhile, Hilda Kahne's overview, issued as a Radcliffe Institute Reprint, is extremely useful as an introduction. For those who are equipped to cope with the technicalities, there is *Economics of the Family* edited by Theodore W. Schultz. We still await the feminist equivalent of Keynes who will scatter the old shibboleths, proclaim the positive advantages of a major shift in the male-female distribution of work, and find a system for attributing worth to unpaid work.

Sociology of work

A third major area of intellectual activity born of the industrialized society is the sociology of work. This includes such subjects as organization theory and comprises the application of concepts of behavioural science, psychology and sociology to organized paid employment.

As we have already seen, a number of women have made distinguished contributions here. However, the literature of the subject, which is vast, presents, at least on preliminary inspection, a curiously sexless approach. One receives the impression that workers are neuter beings. Closer study reveals that this voluminous body of theory is heavily male-oriented. To take an example, in the twenty-three pages of annotated bibliography appended to Alan Fox's *A Sociology of Work in Industry*, there is no reference to any book dealing with women in industry, though there are a number of references to 'how men behave', 'men's orientation to work' and so on. 'Men' and 'man' also feature in the titles of a number of the cited works. When we look at the subjects of detailed studies, we note a concentration on male-dominated areas – automobile manufacture, mining, steelworks and, in the white collar area, management. 'Industrial relations', that is, conflict, receives a lot of attention. In the index to this book, there is no entry under 'women', 'family' or 'children'. The same is true of the index to *Organization Theory*, a book of readings compiled from the works of the major exponents of the subject by D. S. Pugh. Do all these writers actually believe that men and women workers have exactly the same attitudes, motives and general orientation towards paid work in an organized setting? Or, more likely, is it assumed once again that men *are* the industrial workforce? Any tendency to concentrate on males would no doubt be reinforced by the power of patronage of large business organizations who can heavily influence the direction of research, first through decisions on what to fund and, second, through decisions on what field work and experimentation to allow within their own operational units.

Since strikes and other industrial action constitute a major problem for employers, it is not surprising if they show a keen interest in researching the attitudes of the male workers and trade unions concerned. On the other hand, is it not equally worthwhile to examine the reasons for the lesser militancy of women workers, and the similarities and differences between the attitudes of men and women to industrial action?

Dr Ann Oakley, in her book *The Sociology of Housework*, gives her first chapter to 'The Invisible Woman: sexism in sociology'. She begins by pointing out that sociology has never treated housework as work or devoted any study to it. Dealing in general with the sociology of work, she illustrates the invisibility of women employees in the literature of the subject,[33] citing as a rare exception Wild and Hill's study of women in the electronics industry. Notably, she refers to Blauner's passing over of all women workers in the textile industry, that is, nearly half the labour force.[34] Readers are recommended to turn to Dr Oakley's text, which goes on to trace the sexism of sociology to the bias of its founding fathers. Particularly discomforting is her examination of the personally sexist attitudes of these men, and the contrast between Marx's views on the oppression of women and his acceptance of the lifelong sacrifice and subordination of his own wife.[35]

A new, non-sexist approach to the sociology of work is a priority, and one which should clearly be the concern of official equal opportunity agencies. Beyond that, it would appear essential for the sociology of work to include the study of both sexes if the discipline is to make any claim to objectivity. It seems essential also to quarry among the rich insights to be gained from comparing and contrasting the orientation to both paid work and unemployment of women on the one hand and men on the other. If we are indeed approaching an era of chronic high levels of unemployment and shortened working weeks, there must be much to be learned from the study of women workers who typically have a broken pattern of employment, who often work part-time, who have less personal capital invested in paid work and who are worse hit by unemployment.

Specialist studies of women's employment

While women have been largely ignored in the classical literature on sociology of work, specialist studies have been made, which, of course, reinforce the idea of women workers as a race apart and as an element alien to 'real' industry. A review of some publications of the 1960s will serve to illustrate this.

In the late 1950s, Pearl Jephcott and others carried out a two-year study of married women working in a biscuit factory in the East End of London. Part of their findings was released in 1960 in summarized form in the Ministry of Technology booklet entitled rather grandly *Woman, Wife and Worker*. In the context of the steadily increasing number of married women entering the labour market, the booklet sets out to show that employers need not be fearful about the problems of employing married women, especially those with children. These 'problems' stemmed from a stereotype which depicted the married woman as irresponsible and unreliable, much more prone to absenteeism than male workers and liable to resign capriciously and often. The study, and the full-length book based on it, addressed primarily the moral question of whether it was 'right' for married women, and particularly mothers, to go out to work. Thus the question (which seems both sexist and incomprehensible now) – 'Why did these married women work?' elicited the reply, 'Primarily for financial reasons'. This seems obvious to the point of banality, but it was designed to make clear that the object was not to pick up 'pin money' but to make an important contribution to the family budget.[36] Additionally, it was aimed at convincing employers that married women would not regard their jobs capriciously and dodge in and out of work as the fancy took them. The stereotype relates to what Galbraith later identified as the 'convenient social virtue', that is, those women who 'neglect' household duties are to be censured. It also has links back to the nineteenth century when there was great concern about the ill effects on children of their mothers working outside the home. Events in the Second World War also influenced opinion: employers had then been obliged to engage married women in large numbers because of acute labour shortages, but women with children were not subject to the general and stringent official regulations under which labour mobility and absenteeism were restricted. They accordingly acquired a reputation for unreliability. The Min Tech booklet makes no mention of the need for child care facilities (which were provided during the war but closed down afterwards). Nor does it suggest that the 'dual burden' of paid work and domestic work was anything other than an unavoidable necessity.

The Min Tech booklet was reprinted in 1968 (Human Rights Year internationally and the fiftieth anniversary of women's suffrage in Britain) by which time it must have looked slightly out of date. A more positive approach had been shown by the pamphlet 'Labour Turnover' published in 1967 by the Economic Development Committee for the Clothing Industry.[37] Though the question of child care facilities and the 'dual role' are not mentioned, the theme is that the onus is on employers to structure work and evolve personnel policies so as to reduce labour turnover. A number of constructive suggestions are made on selection, training, supervision, pay and other points. Statistics are given which show that it is by no means inevitable that female turnover should be sky high, or even exceed that of male employees.

The 'dual role' is at the heart of Myrdal and Klein's classic study[38] which still repays reading today. While it is written very conscientiously according to orthodox sociological and economic precepts, the perspective is recognizably feminist. Even so, the apologetic note typical of the literature on women working is discernible in a number of passages. Thus in addressing themselves to the question of absenteeism, the

66

authors do not point out that on investigation it might emerge that women are likely to absent themselves for much more responsible reasons than men. Absenteeism has to be admitted as a blemish in women.

Wild and Hill in their study of women in the electronics industry are still posing the question, 'Why do these women work?' but they also attack the stereotype of the woman worker by showing that much of the behaviour which employers object to is caused by the employers' own practices. They attribute most resignations to the lack of satisfying work. Their study, based on a sample of over 2,000 employees, refutes the traditional proposition that women will tolerate monotony well. They criticize the 'de-skilling' of work which treats the employee as if she were a machine. Many women react against the lack of job satisfaction by changing jobs and by absenteeism, thus 'proving' their unreliability. Wild and Hill assessed the annual cost of this turnover to the telecommunications and electronics industries at £5.63 million.

This study illustrates a form of sex discrimination which is not often highlighted – the imposition on women of essentially boring work which does not make use of their capabilities. This is justified by an alleged capacity of women to endure tedium. The work is classified as semi-skilled so that it carries a low rate of pay rather than any compensation for the boredom and depression which it induces. Wild and Hill mention cases where operatives reached a state bordering on mental illness (p. 55).

The EDC pamphlet was dedicated to improving the efficiency and competitiveness of firms in the clothing industry, by better utilization of labour. The massive government study of 1965[39] by Audrey Hunt was prompted by the urgent need to increase the labour force at a time of full employment. The survey, grounded on interviews with women in 10,000 households, was directed to finding ways of enabling more women to enter the labour force. By this time, nearly 50% of all married women held a job, and two-thirds of all women at work were married. Among women responsible for children under sixteen, more than a third were in jobs, and the survey report comments on the child care problem. Echoing the robust views of the biscuit factory women, there is a strong expression of the benefits children gain through their mothers going out to work – in family relationships and in the development of independence as well as in material terms. (The biscuit factory women went further and said that the woman who did not seek a paid job was culpably passing up an opportunity to raise her family's standard of living and was liable to be a muddler in housekeeping. It seems that working class thinking on this issue was ahead of that of the middle class.)

The continuing demand for labour could only be met by an increase in the number of married women taking up employment, and as the 1960s progress there is a shift away from the pleading stance ('We really are acceptable as employees') and the 'women in top jobs' theme appears. Why are there so few women in senior positions? Why are women's qualifications being under-used? These questions were asked by Audrey Hunt, and earlier by Nancy Seear and her collaborators in *A Career for Women in Industry*?[40] This book includes a case study of eight firms and exposes the blatant managerial prejudices against women in line management and senior positions. The first part of the book is a study of the attitudes of grammar school girls to science-based careers. These studies were suggested by a small group of industrialists who approached the London School of Economics and Political Science in 1960. They believed industry was not making good use of women with scientific and technical qualifications. This book firmly establishes the position, of which Seear has been a redoubtable exponent ever since, that sex discrimination constitutes a totally unjustifiable waste of a scarce resource – human talent.

The value of protective legislation was questioned at an OECD seminar in 1968, held at the prompting of the Trades Union Advisory Committee. It was felt that such laws could be 'more of a hindrance than a help'. However, the general introduction says that the unionists wanted the seminar in order to provide factual background which would '*help them in defending the interests of this special group of workers*'. (Stress added.) At the time, women constituted about 35% of the labour force in economically advanced OECD countries and one is reminded of the all too frequent classification of women under 'minorities' in bibliographies, catalogues and other references.

Another general survey was initiated by the UK Committee for Human Rights Year (1968), and was carried out by Pauline Pinder for PEP.[41] Pinder's conclusions are curiously pessimistic considering her work coincided with the emergence of the women's liberation movement. She accepted the 'inevitability' of the dual role and its undesirable consequences for women's careers. She also considered that it was unlikely that the government would introduce equal pay legislation; and she appeared to think legislation an unsuitable remedy for discrimination against women at work, which she described as 'tradition-hallowed'. She concludes that to make progress women will have to 'learn from men how to get what you want in a man's world' – a sentiment totally at odds with the spirit of the new women's movement already emerging powerfully in the United States.

Pinder's survey is especially interesting for its chapter on women's organizations and pressure groups. Her analysis led her to posit the need for a new organization to espouse the interests of all working women, since the fragmented and multifarious pattern of existing organizations was unlikely to achieve effective pressure on those with power to make the necessary changes. Unfortunately this analysis is as true today as it was in 1968.

This brief review of some of the studies of women's employment published in the 1960s illustrates the point that resources for this kind of work are not easily come by. One might take advantage of a special occasion such as Human Rights Year, when it was appropriate to 'do something about women'; or one might persuade government to provide the money in view of perceived national economic needs. Only one of the studies I have mentioned ('A Career for

Women in Industry ?') received direct financial support from industry.

A second point to be made is that all of them start from a negative concept of some kind. None of them deals with women workers as an intrinsically interesting subject, with the possible exception of Myrdal and Klein. There is a great effort to dispel prejudices against women but no suggestion that women have a positive contribution to make. The underlying theme is that women can be as good as men, and that we must remove needless obstacles which impede a woman from putting in the same performance as a man. The self-confidence to proclaim that women had a right to work and that the male-oriented work structure was by no means perfect and could benefit from the contribution of women, was lacking. Tactically, no doubt, it was felt that feminist motivations had better be concealed behind objective scholarship and evidential proofs. In the early 1960s, big was still beautiful and male authority was unlikely to be seriously challenged. Such attitudes were destined to change dramatically and the new women's movement was to play a major role in the new thinking.

3 THE WOMEN'S MOVEMENT

Lepidus	What manner o' thing is your crocodile?
Antony	It is shap'd, sir, like itself, and it is as broad as it hath breadth; it is just so high as it is, and moves with its own organs. It lives by that which nourisheth it, and the elements once out of it, it transmigrates.
Lepidus	What colour is it of?
Antony	Of its own colour too.
Lepidus	Tis a strange serpent.
Antony	Tis so. And the tears of it are wet.
Caesar	Will this description satisfy him?

Shakespeare: Antony and Cleopatra
Act 2, Scene 7

The crocodile was believed to be a fabulous monster generated spontaneously out of the Nile by the operation of the sun. Antony is teasing the rich, but politically insignificant, Lepidus at a drunken party on board ship where political intrigue continues under an appearance of amity; the 'masters of the world', Antony, Caesar and Pompey, the host, have decided on a carve-up of power.

This cameo can be used as a paradigm of the incursion of women's rights questions, the crocodile, into a world which men have ordered to their own satisfaction and where each, temporarily, has received his due. The crocodile is a joke, but it is also a man eater. It lurks, in its excellent camouflage, waiting for a victim.

The most interesting feature of the 'crocodile' however is that it eludes definition. It is what it is and it cannot be classified according to any known categories. This holds good for the contemporary women's movement, too. In terms of formal scholarship and the writing of history, the politics of women's emancipation must be among the most neglected topics, with the least justification for that neglect.

I attempt below analytical description of the movement in terms of the type of politics that we are familiar with. The breadth and diversity of the movement make this a difficult task. Can one find historical analogies?

What happened after women 'won their rights'?

The general history of the women's movement which arose in the last century and culminated in the gaining of votes for women has been recorded and need not be recalled in any detail here. The main aims of the movement, apart from securing the vote, were access to higher education, entry to the professions, and amelioration of the legal status of the married woman, which was subordinated entirely to that of the husband. At the same time, women's trade union activities were important in helping to improve the position of women in manufacturing and service industries.

Looking back now, it is easy to gain the impression that there was a collapse of feminist activity in the inter-war period. It would be truer to say that there was a diffusion of effort. The great campaigns for the vote had united enormous numbers of women and the demonstrations and marches were eye-catching and newsworthy. Once women had won their citizenship and the right to practise most professions, attention focused on the exercise of these rights and on other causes affecting women's welfare. These included the struggle for recognition of birth control, the campaign for reform of the law relating to abortion, pressure for family allowances, and further legislation removing disabilities on women and liberalizing matrimonial law. Many women were deeply involved in the peace movement since they felt that

72

women had a special mission and capacity to influence the world's leaders to outlaw war for ever. In the United States, women provided strong support for prohibition.

The conspicuous success in widely differing endeavours of such women as Marie Curie, Amy Johnson and Margaret Bondfield, and the 'liberation' involved in the 'flapper' fashions, with their short skirts and unconstricting underwear, helped to create the impression that female equality had arrived. It would be a matter of time only before women took their rightful place as equal partners with men in all spheres of life. To this end, many organizations, both national and international, were developed to train women in citizenship, to harness women's enthusiasm for internationalism and the cause of peace, and to press for feminist reforms in countries where women's status was still unsatisfactory.

Through the International Labour Organization, standards were established to prevent the exploitation of women workers and eventually (1951) a convention on equal pay was agreed. National endeavours to secure equal pay continued and in some countries resulted in legislation. The Treaty setting up the European Economic Community contained a clause embodying the principle of equal pay, and the Council of Europe passed resolutions on equal pay and other aspects of women's employment.

These continuing efforts were sustained by established organizations and the older generation of women, including a small number of women legislators. Younger women emerged from the war in the late 1940s and started, or completed, their families. For the middle class woman, life was very different from what it had been before the war. Domestic help was scarce, the use of nannies was frowned on by paediatric experts and, unlike their mothers, this generation had little, if any, leisure to devote to public work and social causes. If they belonged to a woman's organization, it was in order to have one or two afternoons a month for recreation and some company. By the 1960s, the societies which had been created to foster full citizenship and career opportunities for women had largely become social clubs offering artistic and educational opportunities and playing down or ignoring the feminist element in their constitutions. In those organizations which held to a feminist platform, younger women were conspicuously absent. They, and the mothers who bore them during the Second World War and its aftermath, were lost generations as far as the feminist cause was concerned.

The women's movement in terms of political theory

To start with names for the movement: there is an initial difficulty in that we can find no accepted name. The 'women's liberation movement' is often used but is not accepted by all activists, some of whom prefer to speak of 'the women's movement' or even 'feminism'. The apparent parallels here are:

Women's liberation movement	Politically motivated armed resistance to oppression, on the part of outsiders, 'imperialists', by informally organized guerillas. 'Liberation' was used to describe the expulsion by the Allies of the 'Axis' forces from Occupied countries at the end of World War Two; it now has a connotation almost entirely in terms of the politics of the left.
The women's movement	'Movement' here suggests a concatenation of interests which goes beyond, or even excludes, a political dimension: cf. 'the trade union movement'. It also suggests a historical role: one could say that the women's movement dates back at least to the early nineteenth century, which is not true of 'the women's liberation movement'.
Feminism	Defines a point of view, with or without practical consequences. *The*

74

Concise Oxford Dictionary defines it as 'Advocacy, extended recognition, of the claims of women'. *The 20th Century Larousse* gives 'Mouvement d'idées tendant à permettre à la femme d'exercer son activité sociale, économique, politique dans les mêmes conditions que l'homme.' Feminism differs from women's liberation and the women's movement in that men can be feminists, e.g. John Stuart Mill, Frederick Pethick-Lawrence.

Thus we are unclear about a name for this phenomenon, or constellation of phenomena, a demonstration of the fact that it is unclassifiable in terms of male-created political science.

Women grow up in, and inhabit, a political environment created and run by men. It is inevitable that in the early stages of their groping towards an identity of their own, women should define their efforts in terms of those institutions. Thus Mary Wollstonecraft published *A Vindication of the Rights of Woman* in an era (1792) when the rights of man were being widely debated and fought over by men. There were links between the emancipation of slaves in the United States and the women's rights cause. When men struggled for the vote, women did, too; and similarly with the right to work. Today we see women classifying themselves as socialists believing that it is not men who are the oppressors but 'the system'. Some women, though, have run for political office as women's rights candidates, or members of a Parti Feministe, in the last few years, recognizing that no existing party is going to put women's needs and interests in the forefront of its programme.

The typical pattern of revolution goes:
- spread of revolutionary ideas
- attempts to reform by peaceful means from within the system
- frustration of those attempts

- minor outbreaks of violence and/or impatience with slow pace of change
- repression by the ruling class accompanied by continuing violent incidents
- crisis and violent overthrow of existing regime
- period of fighting and chaos
- emergence of new regime in which former revolutionary leaders become the new ruling caste

The first five of these stages were gone through in the British women's suffrage campaign, but at that point World War One occurred and the women's leadership called off operations for the duration. Towards the end of the war, it became clear that women would be granted the vote and resumption of hostilities was not in question. Nor has violence been used to back other demands for such measures as equal pay, liberal abortion laws or free availability of contraceptives.

The literature of contemporary feminism does not contain visions of a women's revolution proceeding through all the stages outlined above to the final domination of men by women. The fighting talk is directed towards raising women's consciousness; they have to stop thinking of themselves as inferior and then they will have the courage and confidence not only to liberate themselves but also to free men from their stereotyped roles, which are built on aggression, toughness and adversarial attitudes.

It is not impossible that if progress towards equality were seriously frustrated for a critically long period, there might be some women who would resort to unconstitutional action, but for women now active in the women's movement or, if not active, convinced of the correctness of the feminist analysis, violent revolution is not on the agenda. (If any pressure was wanted, withdrawal of labour, paid and unpaid, and consumers' strikes, would be more effective than violent outbursts.)

Women are unique among oppressed classes in that they mix with the oppressors, both on intimate terms in marriage and sexual relations, and in close proximity in employment, and in social, artistic, intellectual and sporting activities. Thus a feminist has to think not only about political, legal and economic changes of a general kind, but also how to interpret her feminism in a myriad of everyday relationships with other human beings of all ages and both sexes. This latter aspect of feminism is likely by its nature to be the dominant theme for the individual, since campaigns for legislative changes are intermittent and on the whole far less taxing than the daily application of feminist principles to one's own life and relationships. To define the women's movement or feminist consciousness exclusively, or even primarily, in political terms is an error. Women are re-defining all their attitudes to life and to their own roles. They are finding out what they themselves think and feel, shaking off the dictates of society about what women ought to think and feel, and how they ought to behave.

What is happening has to be related to underlying historical and social trends. These include the astounding changes in the life of women brought about by the control of their own fertility, and by the slow percolation of the effects of what the early feminists secured – political rights, education, the right to work and to practise a profession. For the first time in history, women are able to make choices about the direction of their lives. This involves perception of the whole environment of society and its mechanisms, not as an unalterable system which has to be endured and adapted to, but as an artefact which can be analysed and altered. How have women tackled the task of rediscovering the world?

First, there is the exploration of inner space. More and more women, singly or together (for example, in consciousness raising groups or women's studies courses) are examining their attitudes, prejudices and relationships: how far have they chosen them and how far are they the result of conditioning or moulding by society in its own (hitherto male-dominated) interests? The results of this process are various, and sometimes unattractive to outside observers, but putting aside the more superficial phenomena, they

77

amount to something very important – a definition of womanhood by women on their own terms. This 'revolutionary' activity is not carried on in terms of male categories. On the contrary, it explicitly rejects them, from Freudian psychology to the images of women purveyed by advertisers of consumer goods.

The discoveries or rediscoveries arising from the exploration of woman by woman spread out in many directions – the arts, crafts, health care, religion, psychology, linguistics, sexuality, sport. There is no aspect of life where the reassessment of woman and woman's role cannot 'shake and move'. This should not surprise us, since women form half the human race.

Stemming from a reassessment of what they are, women are also reclaiming the history of what they have been from the male historians. It is being demonstrated that women do have a place even in 'man's history' of dates, events, famous people and 'geniuses who changed the world'. Women may not be numerous among this cast of historical characters but they are beginning to receive their due.

A new type of women's group has come into being to match the new dynamism in feminist consciousness. These groups deliberately reject hierarchical organization, and formal constitutions and procedures based on models evolved in male organizations. What matters is not leadership but full participation by every woman in the group. The older women's organizations, born in the nineteenth and earlier twentieth century, have not been able to attract or absorb the new impetus. Indeed, many of them seem to have become bastions of the female conservatism which they were originally founded to overcome. Instead of equipping women to enter political life, they have provided an escape route into a shadow world of 'women's interests'.

Equally, if not more, significant is the growing number of women who, while not identifying themselves at all closely with feminism or the women's liberation movement, support the basic tenets – that women have a right to self-realization, educational opportunities, economic equality, and control over their own fertility. The disagreements among women are not now about objectives so much as about strategy and tactics. This is not unusual in any broadly based movement which will always have its 'militants' and 'moderates'.

Feminism, after more than a century of activity, has finally become respectable. It is now only a minority who still grumble about, but cannot act against, overt expressions of women's right to exercise their capabilities equally with men in all spheres. Internationally, this received an imprimatur in International Women's Year. Nationally and regionally, it is reflected in legislation, official reports, the setting up of equal opportunity commissions and in a thousand other similar official or semi-official manifestations. These normative statements are not to be confused with the actual achievement of equality: their importance lies in their declaration of public policy and their inauguration of officially approved efforts to speed up the progress towards equality.

Opposition from women to women's liberation

Most of the visible, articulate opposition to the women's liberation movement comes from women. In the United States, it has become organized in a campaign against the Equal Rights Amendment to the Constitution. Specific measures do not arouse the same opposition. The campaign for the British Sex Discrimination law, for example, was supported by all the traditional women's organizations and the only opposition was from those ambitious spirits who thought the Bill did not go far enough. The ERA, however, sweeps away all legislative sex discrimination of whatever kind and the campaign against it is a rallying point for those who fear and mistrust the whole notion of 'liberation' and its repudiation of old-fashioned 'femininity'.[42]

In Europe, there is no comparable constitutional campaign of such wide-ranging impact. Opposition to the women's movement is much more diffuse and takes the form of individual pronouncements by women in public (eagerly reported), or in private, censuring the behaviour of professed members of the movements. Criticism is rarely extended to the basic principles of the movement. Usually, one suspects, the critics would be unable to enumerate them: in any case, they are quite unexceptionable (unless one holds a religious position on abortion). The more frequently voiced objections are to the style, language and aggressive behaviour of liberationists. (Putting men down in public, for example.) Use of 'male' swear words is felt to be distasteful and offensive. Accusations against the women's movement are that the aim is to 'force' all women to go out to work, 'dumping' their children in 24-hour nurseries; that they are 'against men', and if not all lesbian, at any rate do not give heterosexuality the primacy it deserves; and that they are aligned with the far left in politics. It would be simple to defuse these caricatures and show them to be inaccurate, but it is more interesting here to consider the basis of the criticisms. At one level, there is the usual shrinking away from anything unconventional, but in view of the great variety of unconventional behaviour people see around them and on television, it can hardly explain the particular repugnance to women's liberationists. One explanation is that a snap dismissal of the whole women's movement on the grounds of unladylike behaviour and political extremism relieves the critics from any obligation to examine the serious issues which the movement addresses. Possibly critics even envy the free behaviour and outspokenness of the women they criticize, but dare not openly praise or copy it; their criticism would then serve the purpose of allaying any suspicions among their families and associates that they might be fellow-travellers with the movement.

A distressing phenomenon is the tendency among women who do support the cause of sex equality to go out of their way to disassociate themselves from the movement or, rather, the media-fostered image of a disreputable, foul-mouthed and ludicrous band of women on the fringes of society. Interviewers seem to take particular care to put women on the spot with a question such as, 'Would you call yourself a "women's libber"?'[43] It is difficult to make an adequate response to this. Knowing the poor image associated with 'women's lib', the great majority of subjects succumb to the temptation to disdain any connection with it. (It is rarely possible to get the interviewer to report, or give air time to, a disquisition on what the women's liberation movement really is.) A better tactic is to answer 'Yes', thus throwing the interviewer off balance and demonstrating that you are not frightened to the threat of a smear; then quickly explain that that means you are in favour of equal opportunity at work and in education, equal pay, etc., etc.

Unlike the militant suffragettes, modern activists rarely break the law. Their offence is to be seen acting out a total repudiation of the traditional image of women or, more accurately, 'ladies', wives and mothers as the nineteenth century idealized them. Since women have been conditioned to cherish their image and live up to it, the sight of other women smashing it in public is deeply shocking.

Do women oppose the women's movement on grounds of self-interest? That is, do they resist the idea that marriage is not a 'meal ticket for life', that 'chivalry' or extra politeness to women is condemned? Do they think it unjust that a divorcee with means should contribute to the maintenance of her ex-husband, or to children in the husband's care? I think these aspects raise fears and resentments, particularly among older women who have given their whole lives to home-making; but the developments we are considering are the result of the evolution of matrimonial law and social customs over a century or more and cannot be ascribed to the effect of a movement which emerged in the 1960s.

Essentially neither the contemporary women's movement nor its predecessors going back into the last century are adequately understood by the overwhelming majority of citizens of either sex. These movements have not been taught as part of history and civics in schools and universities, whereas the education system leaves no-one in any doubt about how men won their political rights. Each fresh phase, therefore, tends to be seen as an isolated phenomenon. There has been a failure of popular journalism and broadcasting to explain or even adequately describe the movement. Serious treatment is confined to the better quality press and, increasingly, to the specialist journals and newsletters set up by women themselves. The traditional women's organizations, many of them created by pioneering women around the turn of the century, many designed to follow up the success of the suffrage campaigns, seem to have done little or nothing to educate their members in the history and continuing endeavours of the women's movement. Until the recent creation of women's studies courses, no other organization has felt any responsibility or interest in supplying this need.

Women's criticisms of the women's movement of the kind I have described cannot be taken as invalidating it. In a sense, they demonstrate how necessary it is. Insofar as they are based on inadequate knowledge they can be discounted. Protests and opposition based on fear, which in turn is based on lack of information and understanding should be obviated as far as possible. This is a responsibility of the women's movement; however, its resources are minute, and if governments mean what they say about sex equality and equal opportunity, they need to invest in making more information available so that debate can be conducted along informed and reasonable lines, and equal opportunity policies can be realized, unhindered by misguided opposition.

Do men have any part to play in the women's movement?

The early women's movement had its male adherents. In Britain, there was a Men's League for Women's Suffrage and a number of Parliamentarians and others who espoused the cause. It is difficult to think of any well-known men who have publicly supported the 'new' women's movement as a whole although there are male legislators who will join the campaigns for specific reforms such as laws on equal opportunity. There are some informal male groups supporting women's liberation, and the new women's movement has led to the formation of men's liberation groups in which men seek to express and, if possible, free themselves from the constraints which stereotyping and the conventional sex roles have thrust on them. Some feminist organizations offer membership to men (on equal terms with women, not as associate members be it noted!) but the recently formed women's groups exclude men, as the traditional women's organizations do, though for different reasons.

In view of the low level of support from men on the one hand and their record of virulent, persistent and abusive opposition to women's attempts to improve their status on the other, it is not surprising that women activists should be chary of men, even those who appear to offer help and support. Some women in long-established feminist organizations, however, make a point of stressing that feminism is not a battle in which women want to beat down and subject men to disadvantages, but a branch of human rights, aimed at improving life for all. They insist that there should be men speakers at conferences, and that men as well as women should be invited as guests of honour at social functions. (Women's liberationists are more likely to express the brotherhood of men by getting a men's group to run a creche at a women's seminar.) Nevertheless, I do not believe that even these women truly accept that men can be active feminists in the full sense; just as a white person can have liberal views but cannot genuinely share the struggles of coloured minorities. The real revolution has to take place in women's mind and spirit and it will happen, and is happening, irrespective of men's support, opposition or apathy.

Opposition, in fact, can help to rouse women's indignation about their second-class citizenship and thus increase the strength of the movement. The primary question for men, then, is not whether they can or should support the women's movement, but (as the emergence of the men's liberation groups suggests) how they can adapt to the changes it is bringing about, and take advantage of what it offers in terms of opportunities to break out of constricting attitudes about sex and gender. It is difficult, perhaps impossible, for women to help men do this: intrinsically, the situation precludes the traditional supportive female behaviour which buoys up the man and makes him feel he's not such a bad guy. Perhaps the best that women can do is grit their teeth, stand aside and watch the men painfully working it out on their own, and then join the loving celebrations when the men have made a significant advance. Sometimes one hears women say that they are sorry for men, having to face up to the changes in sex roles. Why should we be sorry for someone who has the chance to rid himself of archaic delusions and to relate to others and himself far more enjoyably and comfortably than before? Perhaps it is even rather patronizing for women to feel sorry for men in this situation – do they think men are too feeble and immature to cope?

If it is difficult to see men as feminists in the full sense, that is not to say that men cannot play a significant and useful part in many practical ways. They can, for example, do excellent work convincing traditionally minded women who are afraid of liberation that they are behind the times and worrying needlessly, and that they will not lose their 'femininity'[44] if they come out in support of equal rights and generally speak up for themselves. Men could also put up a very effective resistance to the demeaning and obscene treatment of women in all forms of media, including common speech, swear words and jokes. In both these examples, action by men would obtain results quicker than representations by women alone.

The women's movement and employment issues

The engineering factory where I worked during the autumn and winter of 1976/77 offered little comfort to one who had been an enthusiastic campaigner for the Sex Discrimination Act 1975. Located in a conservative and, in industrial relations terms, non-militant area of the North-East, it displayed sex-segregation of employment throughout all its departments and functions without a single exception. The place

84

might have been designed especially to illustrate the division of the labour market. 'Women's work' involved 'manual dexterity' and was mainly performed sitting down at benches No woman employee was classified as 'skilled'. There was no female chargehand and all foremen were male. In the white collar sections there were some women with considerable experience of the business, but not one female supervisor or executive. At the beginning of my six months' tour of duty, personnel work was in the hands of an unqualified woman on temporary secondment from another factory belonging to the same group, the former male personnel manager having succumbed to a severe illness; while I was there, she was replaced by a new, qualified, male personnel manager.

The only women with any position of authority were two shop stewards representing the women operatives. One of these was prepared to make occasional forays into the man's world. During a period of slackness, when the women were kept idle for days on end, she had done some machining in the 'men's' section rather than endure the endless chat and magazine reading in the women's rest room; and during my stay, she had not only entered the local dominoes championship as the first woman contestant ever, but got through to the final. The other shop steward was a younger woman with a small child who worked part time. Both women were concerned about projected changes in the piece-work system, which enabled some women to earn more than some of the lower-paid men employees. However, a deeper preoccupation was the possibility that machines, some of which were already installed but not fully operative, would automate much of the existing 'women's work' leaving only 'specials' to be done by hand – that is, jobs with a non-standard specification or small batch work not worth putting on a machine designed for long runs. Neither woman thought in terms of opening up 'men's work' to women, though the work done by men was not particularly heavy or arduous on the whole.

All this was far removed from the petitioning and banner-carrying, the drafting of evidence to Parliamentary committees and the excitement of the packed gallery as the Sex

Discrimination Bills came and went in the House of Commons – in all of which I had enthusiastically participated, along with hundreds of other women and their representative organizations. It was far, too, from the blue collar heroines I had learnt about in the United States, women who had defied both management and unions and claimed their legal right to equal employment opportunity. They battled against harassment and lentghy court procedures, and eventually won through, supported by women's rights activists and women lawyers.

The new women's movement emerged at a time when equal pay was, in principle, gaining some ground. Legislation had been passed in a number of countries, and signatories to the ILO Convention were increasing in number. A requirement for equal pay was included in the Treaty of Rome setting up the European Economic Community. However, it was clear that an equal pay entitlement is not much good when women are employed in 'women's work' which cannot be equated with the more highly paid 'men's work'. The requirement is sometimes expressed in terms of 'equal value' but this is difficult to establish when the kinds of work are very different.

A first priority for the new movement was therefore to campaign for equal opportunity so that the sex segregation of the labour market could be broken down. In the United States, indignation at the ineffectiveness of the Equal Employment Opportunities Commission led in 1966 to the formation of the National Organization for Women, a powerful expression of the new feminism, and ultimately to the strengthening of the relevant laws and dramatic measures for enforcement against major corporations. Legislation in other countries is too recent for one to predict whether a similar chain of events will occur there.

In the employment sphere, there was much in common between the objectives of the younger women who identified with the new movement and the older women who had fought the battles on equal pay. In Britain, all sections of the women's movement joined together to campaign for equal opportunity legislation in the early 1970s and there was a tremendous united upsurge of protest when the government of the day issued proposals for tax reform under which the state 'family allowance', paid in cash to the mother since its inception in 1945, would be credited to the father. For women who were not in paid employment, this weekly allowance in respect of the children was the only money they could legally call their own. (In English law a wife has only the right to be suitably maintained by her husband and there is no community of property; she has no right to know what her husband's income is, and thus can make no proper assessment of what a 'suitable' level of maintenance might be.)

A claim which arose from the movement was for 'wages for housework': women's unrecognized contribution to the economy should be properly rewarded. This could be argued on quasi-Marxist grounds, in that women serviced the workers on whose efforts capitalism depended, but it has also attracted favourable attention from middle-class women who think that they should not be penalized for giving up their earning power in order to devote themselves to domestic duties while their children are small. Thus we see the subject aired in a glossy homemakers' magazine (Edmunds, op.cit.) and interest is kept alive by repeated references to the 'worth of a wife' in the press, based on court cases and insurance companies' estimates. Many feminists argue against wages for housework, as a means of fettering women even more closely to housework: and why should couples be rewarded by the state for adopting a lifestyle which reduces their contribution to the economy? These feminists would agree with the views of the Bermondsey biscuit factory women about the stay-at-home wife.

The women's movement has also had some effect on the trade union movement or, rather, there are women trade unionists who count themselves as members of the women's movement. Like women in political groups of the Marxist or socialist persuasion, women trade unionists are caught up in a structure created to serve male ends which, while paying lip service to female equality, does very little, if anything, to advance it. While socialist women seem to agonize about the conflict of loyalties or the schismatic theology this entails, women unionists appear to be free of such hang-ups, perhaps because they are so immersed in practical tasks. In the United States, labour union women formed their own Confederation dedicated to improving the status of women workers. In Britain, an important debate continues about the need for the continued existence of the separate annual assembly of women unionists associated with the Trades Union Congress. (Women unionists also have access to the annual conference of the TUC but the proportion of women attending is small.) The benefits of amalgamation of a women's enterprise with a male or mixed system are questionable, and it is to be hoped that the danger of the women's TUC being dissolved has now passed.

Older women trade unionists at the top of the movement probably continue to view 'women's liberation' somewhat askance, and on the shop floor there is a feeling that the women's movement is a middle class affair remote from the problems of women wage earners. In the United States, on the other hand, blue collar women pioneered in bringing cases under the equal opportunity law. Legislation gradually has an educational effect: when its implementation is the concern of both management and trade unions, through their action women will become aware of the issues.

Pressures to bring 'women's issues' to the centre of industrial relations will continue. In 1975, the British Trades Union Congress passed a resolution proposed by the Tobacco Workers Union emphasizing the importance of a liberal abortion law. As a result of this incorporation of an abortion policy in the TUC's official stance, the TUC took action when the Abortion Act 1967 was threatened by a private member's Bill seeking to narrow its scope. Unions in the United States have put much effort into obtaining adequate maternity leave provisions. In 1978, a coalition of Swiss women's groups began a campaign for improved maternity provision, including the right (on Swedish lines) for either mother or father to take nine month's paid leave after the birth of their child.

Before we go on to examine government action on questions relating to women's employment, we should look at the state of the labour market today. Where does 'women's work' stand now? And what is its present relation to 'men's work'?

4 THE LABOUR MARKET TODAY

Much information is available in books, newspapers and published official statistics on the sex segregation of the labour market in industrialized countries. Women remain in sectors of employment strongly associated with the traditional six tasks. Curiously, the ancient constraint on women's leaving home for any length of time also lingers. There is still a widespread belief that women can't travel on business. An outstanding example of this type of attitude was unearthed by the equal opportunity programme consultants Boyle Kirkman Associates of New York: they found that one client firm's computer had been programmed to print 'No' on all female employees' personnel records in answer to a question about willingness to relocate. The women themselves had not had the question put to them. The new areas of women's work are those which have been created by technological advances. The most notable are clerical work, where women came into business to work the new-fangled telephones and typewriting machines (and later, computers), and electrical and electronic manufacturing where the traditional attribution of 'manual dexterity' secured employment for women in delicate assembly work and wiring.

Women are the growth element in the labour force
In the last quarter century, a period of unprecedented economic growth and rising living standards in industrialized countries, the demand for additional labour has been met by

the entry of more women, and particularly married women, into paid employment.

To take some examples of OECD statistics, the proportion of women in the labour force rose in the years 1954 to 1975 in Australia from just over 20% to 34.2%; in Canada between 1950 and 1975 from just over 20% to 35.5%; and in the USA in that period from just under 30% to 39.6%. The percentages of women aged 25–59 who were in the labour market (the female 'participation rate') in those countries in 1975 were: Australia 46.8%, Canada 43.8% (ages 25–64); and USA 53.9%. These female participation rates can be compared with others at the same period – Italy 31.3%, West Germany 48.8% (1974), France 55.2%, Denmark 68.2%, Sweden 72.4% and Finland 75.5%. The proportion of women in the West German labour force stayed static between 1964 (37.2%) and 1975 (37.7%) – possibly this reflects the employment of the *Gastarbeiter* (immigrant workers). In Japan, the proportion has decreased slightly in the last twenty years and stood at 37.4% in 1975; however the participation rate was quite high – 52.7% – in 1974. The trend may perhaps be due to increased automation of work formerly done by women. Italy also had had a static proportion – 28.2% in 1964, 28.1% in 1975 and a low participation rate – 31.3% – in 1975. I would not venture to embark on any detailed interpretation of these statistics, but it is clear that the general trend has been for the proportion of women workers to increase in the OECD countries.

Changes in employment of married women

An idea of the dramatic change in the married woman's part in paid employment is discernible from Swedish statistics: in 1930, only 9% of married women were gainfully employed and by 1945 there had not been much change – the figure was 11%. Thereafter it rose rapidly and reached 53% in 1971. In the early 1970s about 50% of Swedish mothers with pre-school age children were in the labour market.[45] In Great Britain in 1971, 46.7% of married women in the age group

20–24, and 38.4% of those aged 24–29 (the most likely to have pre-school age children), were participating in the labour market.[46] (But in Scotland, only 17% of married women with children under five were in paid employment.[47] In 1971, married women formed 23.1% of the British labour force as against 13.7% in 1951.[48] In Denmark, comparable figures were 25.6% in 1971 and 12.2% in 1960. The increase in the Danish labour force in that period was almost wholly accounted for by the recruitment of married women.[49]

The expectation is that these trends will continue, and latest figures in the Eurostat series confirm that, despite the major recession, the proportion of women in the labour force continues to grow. This is to be expected since it is a corollary of demographic trends – earlier marriage, falling birthrate, planned families of small size. Highly developed economies show a marked tendency to expand service jobs and decrease manufacturing and basic industry jobs. This means both that there are more opportunities for women, since service work is largely 'women's work', and also that more and more of the tasks which used to be done in the home are performed by outside agencies, thus freeing women to spend more hours in paid employment. It also means that the core of traditional 'men's work' is shrinking. This trend will be accentuated by the development of micro-processor applications in industry.

There are more job opportunities for women, and they are finding themselves able to respond to these opportunities. That, as they say, is the good news, and the rest of the statistical picture is the bad news.

Women worse hit by unemployment

When it comes to unemployment, women are more affected than men. Let us recall some of the figures for women's proportion of the labour force and compare them with their proportion in the registered unemployed according to Eurostat figures. (The recession was precipitated by events in 1973.)

	1975		1977	
	% women in labour force	% women among registered unemployed	% women in labour force	% women among registered unemployed
West Germany	37.7	42.0	37.9	49.8
Italy	28.1	36.7	30.6	39.0
Belgium	34.4	52.3	34.7	59.5
Denmark	41.6	29.3	42.3	42.2
UK*	38.8	20.5	39.3	27.9

Source: OECD and Eurostat statistics

*The United Kingdom has an untypical system in that married women have been able to opt out of paying full social security insurance: as a result they forfeit unemployment benefit and therefore tend not to register as unemployed. It has been estimated that up to half of women looking for jobs may therefore be missing from the unemployment statistics.

Note that the position has deteriorated between 1975 and 1977. Between 1976 and 1977, male unemployment in the EEC increased by 6.8% and and female unemployment by 15.4%. The underlying factors are examined in an article by Diane Werneke in the International Labour Review.[50] One of the leading causes identified by Werneke is the concentration of women's employment in a narrow range of jobs, often of an unskilled or semi-skilled nature. This meant that unemployed women found it harder to get another job, a difficulty which was compounded by their lack of adequate education and training. Thus while the recession tended to manifest itself initially in the sphere of 'men's work', as time went by the other sectors, in which women worked, were severely affected. Werneke points out that while male employment picked up in the recovery phase of 1975–76, conditions for females became worse in Belgium and the United Kingdom, two of the four countries she examined.

The crowding of women into a small number of occupations is at the root of much of their unsatisfactory position. The occupations in question have a strong connection with the six tasks, but have been expanded through the introduction of new technology, as we have already seen. This 'ghetto' phenomenon is vividly illustrated in Shaeffer and Axel's excellent chart book[51] documenting the situation in the United States. 1970 census data showed that 82% of all female workers were in four occupational categories – 35% clerical, 17% service workers, 14% semi-skilled operative and 16% professionals and technicians (which includes teaching and the 'caring professions'). For men, four categories (craft, operative, professional and managerial) comprised 65% of those employed, leaving 35% spread over the remaining seven categories.

A breakdown within the categories shows women filling most of the jobs in teaching, librarianship, nursing, social work, low level office work, telephone operating, packing, garment making, textile operations, cooking, waiting and the health service. The British 1971 Census shows a similar picture – 61% of women employed in ten occupations including clerical, service, shop assistants and other retail, cleaners, teachers, nurses and textile operatives. In Sweden in 1971, five categories of work employed 55% of women workers – health, office work, shop assistants, domestic and reception work, and caretaking and house-cleaning. In the same year in the Republic of Ireland, 71% of women worked in four job categories – clerical, professional and technical, service, and commerce, insurance and finance. Of the other nineteen categories, four had no women at all, and only three – agriculture, textiles, and transport and communication had any substantial representation of women (i.e. above 2%). Cornu, from whose report I have taken these figures, makes it clear that the agriculture figures are somewhat understated owing to 'the Census convention of not classifying farmers' wives as "gainfully employed".'

Pay and other conditions are not equal

Most people are aware that equal pay legislation has not brought about equal pay in practice. This, again, is to a great extent due to the sex segregation of jobs so that there are few areas where women's work can be directly compared with men's work. As we also know, women do not have more leisure to compensate for their inferior pay. Aspects of taxation can help or hinder – in Canada a mother who is in paid employment can deduct child care expenses in computing her taxable income; in Sweden there has been separate taxation of husband and wife since 1971, and as a transitional provision a tax credit was allowed for wives not in paid employment. Pension arrangements often favour men, and their widows. If women's retiring age is earlier, they have less time than men in which to scale the organization's career ladder, a disadvantage compounded by the fact that they will often have reached the lower rungs later in life, too. As women live longer, why cannot they opt to work to a greater age than men? In some countries, account is taken in the state pension scheme of years spent by a woman in child-rearing. There are different attitudes in different countries about whether actuarial rectitude requires lower pension benefits for women[52] and higher premia from women who take out personal health insurance. Fringe benefits for managers are male-oriented: many women might prefer provision of help in the home or labour-saving equipment to a company car. (What about a company robot for women executives?) What is the privilege of lunching in the executive dining room worth if your lunch hours are devoted to shopping and other domestic errands?

Women are not in a position to influence the future

If conditions are not satisfactory now, as these examples illustrate, nor are women well represented in the power structures – government, management and trade union officialdom – which are shaping conditions for the future. There are some encouraging developments: more women graduates are going into industry in specialisms formerly all-male in Britain, and while none of our top twenty companies has a woman director, in the United States 28% of manufacturing companies and 41% of non-manufacturing companies have women board members.[53] However, in the main women are not in positions of strategic importance and many, perhaps most, of those few who are, do not include an understanding of the women's movement or of equal opportunity law and its implementation among their qualifications. Many of them have internalized the values and attitudes of their male colleagues and perhaps quite unconsciously have dissociated themselves from the great majority of their sex. They can be more harsh and prejudiced against women than men are.

This can be illustrated by two items of information. First, the results of a study by a leading British manufacturer in the pharmaceutical industry. This company had a policy of promoting women and men on an equal opportunity basis into responsible posts in its personnel department. The decisions of these appointees were monitored over ten years and it was found that the women personnel managers recommended fewer women staff for promotion, or for appointment to their own units, than their male colleagues. Second, there is information bearing on this point in a survey carried out among women in senior management in 1977 by Alfred Marks Bureau Limited, a major private sector employment agency in Britain. Out of a sample of 316, 63% thought that few women had the capacity or desire to hold senior posts in their company, and the survey report quotes dismissive remarks about women by surveyed individuals such as, 'The majority of criticisms made by men of women are true.' 34% were positively against the women's movement, and while 38% were in favour of it, only 4% were active in it.

These findings betray a deep insecurity about the position of women in business. One's position is so tenuous, it seems, that only the most superlatively able women can be allowed into senior management, women who are beyond the reach of the most captious male critic. Less qualified or able women,

women who will not, or do not, play the game the men's way, must be eliminated, or denounced as inefficient by those women who have made it, lest the hardly won and precariously held ground be lost.

Salvation will not be brought about by the beleaguered 'top women'. Let us look at the change agents which have been specifically appointed to the task of equalizing opportunities.

5 ELIMINATING SEX SEGREGATION IN EMPLOYMENT

Many efforts have been made nationally and internationally to bring 'women's work' in paid employment up to the standards of 'men's work'. In the second half of our century endeavours have been directed towards a new objective – namely, obliterating the barriers between these two sex-determined sectors of employment.

Work is already unisex technically

In one sense, most of these barriers have already disappeared, in that technical advance has eroded those traditional areas of employment where the need for physical strength and the requirement to endure harsh working conditions resulted in the work being automatically classified as 'men's'. Nancy Seear has often cited the exercise undertaken some years ago in a Swedish steelworks, where it was concluded, after an analysis of the content of all jobs in the plant, that there was only one which could not be equally well undertaken by a person of either sex. Comparisons with other countries show us that the definitions of men's and women's work are not the same everywhere. Thus, in Japan, women work in ship-building, in Russia they are engineers, in Nigeria they play a dominant role in the trading of goods and commodities. During both World Wars, there have, of course, been in-numerable examples of women doing 'men's work'.

If we are not already at the point where, technically speaking, all jobs are actually or potentially unisex, we are very

near it. Technology can now be used to give choice
job content, rather than dictating it. In the past, human
had to deploy their efforts in overcoming the intra
nature of their environment. Early industrialization req
people to serve the machines. Nature had been a hard t..sk-
master, and so was the machine-assisted manufacturing system. Employees had to adapt to this system, and its economic implications. Industrial injuries, occupational diseases,
insecurity of employment, low and fluctuating levels of pay
were accepted as natural misfortunes, the result of the same
inexorable laws of existence which produced famine, plague
and other disasters. The idea that humans can control their
environment, rather than merely reacting and suffering, is a
very new one in human history, and one which is not completely assimilated yet. This idea is vital to the design of jobs,
and it is one of the keys to the transformation of the labour
market from the sex-segregated to a unisex mode.

We have the technical ability, then, to implement a full
equal opportunity programme but we are far from achieving
such a programme at present. What are the obstacles in our
way, and what are the instruments which we are using to
displace those obstacles?

Impediments to equal opportunity?

Whether or not a society has laws designed to give women
equal employment opportunity, it is unlikely explicitly to
reject the principle of equal opportunity nowadays. Numerous inter-governmental organizations, including the United
Nations, have agreed on formal statements of this principle,
and of the twin principle of equal pay. What are the factors
impeding the realization of what has been publicly recognized
as desirable?

First, there is not the political will to bring about the necessary changes. There is no doubt we could set up the programmes, allocate the finance and arrange for the education
of public opinion, if we wanted to. However, it has to be
recognized that such programmes would be among the

biggest that governments had ever attempted short of mobilizing the whole population in time of war. The time span of such programmes would outlast the life of any government or legislature. The action would affect almost every member of the population of working age, and would also require radical changes in education and training. By some it would be seen as a zero sum gain – what women gained, men would lose. This would not be the case, for the reasons adduced by Samuelson, but educational effort would be needed to counteract factors which might lead to a backlash.

Thus the scale of the enterprise is daunting, and since men are in control of the mechanisms of power, they are unlikely to devote massive resources to an equal employment opportunity programme unless there is strong pressure from women electors and their male allies. Such pressure has produced some results in a number of countries but nothing yet on the scale required. The severe recession experienced in the 1970s has made it more difficult to put across equal opportunity policies.

The second major factor inhibiting progress towards equal opportunity is the extremely low levels of participation by men, and boys, in domestic tasks and child care within the family. While women have done all types of 'men's work' at one time or other, there is little reciprocal movement of men into 'women's work' of the unpaid sort which keeps the world turning. The way in which men's refusal to do domestic work can sabotage even an enlightened attempt to give equal opportunity to women is illustrated by the story of the Israeli kibbutz movement.

Tiger and Shepher's wide-ranging survey *Women in the Kibbutz* is based on detailed examination of a mass of statistics compiled over the years within the kibbutz movement. From the early years of this century, the movement's founders, influenced by Marxist and socialist ideas, determined that women should have an equal role in production with men, thus ensuring them an equal share in the 'dignity of labour'. In the pioneering days, this philosophy was carried into practice to some extent. This was facilitated by the very small number of children and the drastic simplification of 'service' work in primitive conditions. Nevertheless, in practice service work was always regarded as primarily women's work, with men and boys helping on a temporary basis. Men never undertook the care of children. The maturity of the settlements brought with it a considerable increase in service work as living standards rose and child-rearing became a normal part of kibbutz life. Women at first protested at being moved out of production but to no avail, and the doom of the equality ideal was sealed by the unwillingness of men to engage in service work. Moreover, boys brought up in the kibbutz are not trained to do 'women's work'. (It should be noted that there is no financial advantage in production work – all members of a kibbutz have equal financial status.) The end of the development has been a division of labour more sex-segregated than that of Israeli society in general, paralleled by equivalent sex segregation in the various organizing committees which are an essential feature of kibbutz life, and reflected also in the lower participation of women in the governmental aspects of the settlements. This occurred despite repeated exhortations from the federations (into which kibbutzim are affiliated) to ensure equal participation by women.

Tiger and Shepher advance various reasons for the non-realization of the consciously pursued ideal of the equality of the sexes, none of which they regard as sufficient. Unfortunately, their research focused on women only and they did not investigate male attitudes and behaviour. They come to the conclusion (which could be thought anti-feminist) based on biological and evolutionary themes that women in the kibbutz positively prefer a lifestyle which involves maximum contact with children. This does not give any weight to the evidence that women actively protested against being relegated to service tasks. Women who came into kibbutzim after the pioneering stage did not form their own feminist ethic – the ideal of equality was therefore largely held up by a male-dominated system. One can also point out that there were no rewards for complying with the equality policy and no sanctions for non-compliance. If men mainly refused to do service work, it was inevitable that women would have to do it as the volume increased.

It is not clear from Tiger and Shepher's book what rewards men gain by insisting on production jobs but despite the absence of monetary advantage one can imagine that prestige and possibly more congenial working hours are among the benefits. The whole ethic of the kibbutz is founded on the moral value of productive work and those who carry it out must accordingly have a high status.

The question of sharing domestic tasks is not merely one of fair behaviour within marriage. The whole paid employment structure is based on the assumption that men will have domestic support services provided by their womenfolk. Men's career pattern, and the personnel policies that go with it, are all underpinned by women's unpaid services, and by the poorly remunerated support of women employees. For men, the idea of dismantling this highly convenient, life-long service, comes into the category of thinking the unthinkable. I happen to know from personal experience just how good this kind of service makes one feel, how expansive. There was a short time in 1973–74 when I had both an excellent secretary at work and a highly efficient part-time aide at home. I had hired the latter because of a large workload associated with a voluntary enterprise I was helping to start up. For a brief period, I experienced something of the support that most men command all their lives, and I can fully understand why the thought of losing it is anathema. (However the idea of having someone perform the same services for me 'for love' is repugnant.)

The third major reason for the lack of significant progress towards equal opportunity is insufficiency of ideology and theoretical groundwork, which is a factor towards which this book is addressed. Spontaneous popular movement is not enough – there has to be a well-articulated thought system which can inform the demands for change, and carefully designed techniques for bringing that change about. Violent revolution is not an option for the vast majority of women:

they want orderly, well-planned changes which will benefit them here and now, not just accrue for future generations. Most women, contrary to media slurs, do not want men to be subjected to serious indignity or financial detriment as a result of things being put right for women. The women's movement thus presents the first major challenge to the capacity of the human race to make nation-wide, planned, uncoercive changes in social organization. (The efforts in some developing countries to control the growth of population by popularizing contraception are comparable but not of the same order.)

A fourth factor which makes change hard to achieve is that so much of 'women's work', stemming from the basic six tasks, is unpaid or very badly paid. We are aware of the difficulties of creating a common currency for the countries of the European Economic Community, which arise from the unequal economic development within and between those countries. The problem with 'men's work' and 'women's work' is a hundred times worse. Men and women simply do not inhabit the same economic order, and it is therefore extremely difficult to envisage an integration of the economic position of the two sexes starting from where we are now. This is one reason for the importance of the 'wages for housework' debate: it is about getting women on to the same economic footing as men. As long as half the work women do has no recognized measurable economic value which can be compared with what men do the debate about equal pay is missing a vital dimension. While women, and men, who work for each other, and for their children and other dependants, are often motivated by affection and enjoyment of family life, it is an entirely different thing to say that women (and only they) *ought* to do this work for nothing, that they should feel perpetually guilty if they devote time to building an economic base of their own. 'The choice' (between staying at home and going out to work) for which so many women stipulate, even in the women's movement, is no choice but a trap. What it means is that some women (mainly in the professional and managerial classes) want to preserve their 'right' not to take on the dual burden of paid work and domestic responsibilities; they want to avoid the guilt of feeling, or being made to feel, that they are sacrificing their families to their careers. One could hardly blame them for this, but the ability to opt out of what is seen as an intolerable situation is not a true choice. While one can sympathize with those women who think a dual role is beyond them, one must recognize that 'the choice' allows scope for undesirable pressure from husbands and other members of the family dissuading a woman from embarking on paid employment; it enables some women, who could in fact without strain contribute to the economy, to skive under the pretence of fulfilling domestic duties; and it encourages women in the belief (already inculcated by social conditioning) that society does not expect them to make the same effort as men to develop and use their talents. 'Just a housewife' is self-deprecatory, but it is also an unshakeable alibi – it shows, as J. K. Galbraith might put it, maximum possession of the 'convenient social virtue'. 'The choice' – so innocuous, so right in a democratic society, so appropriate to the western industrialized system which boasts that its whole rationale is giving the people choice rather than what the State finds it convenient for them to have – 'the choice' is one of the greatest obstacles to improving the position of women. A critical examination of the ideology of 'the choice' and a policy for handling it, eliminating it or transforming it, is urgently needed. Equal opportunity agencies could be commissioning research on these lines.

The fifth factor is lack of technical expertise in creating and implementing programmes for equal opportunity and affirmative action. In the United States, this expertise has had to be built up very rapidly and there are now people in employing organizations or acting as consultants who have considerable experience of running such programmes. There are also lawyers who specialize in equal opportunity cases. The Equal Employment Opportunities Commission has a fund of experience and employs experts of various kinds. It has a long series of detailed statistics from individual employers. It would be to the advantage of equal opportunity agencies to create a network so that they can share their knowledge and ideas. Why not found an international journal of equal opportunity laws and practice?

Governmental action for equal opportunity

Behind the national sex discrimination laws emerging in the 1970s lies much work done by international organizations This is not to say that the international work precipitated the passing of national laws (though it has in the EEC) but it was important in making the question of sex discrimination in employment a familiar and respectable one and it also led to the collection, collation and publication of multitudes of statistics relating to the position of women in paid employment. Putting the subject on the agendas of governments and their officials is a vital step. International Women's Decade 1975–85 has been set up by the United Nations to facilitate the monitoring of progress towards the goals set out in the World Plan of Action. This was drawn up at the 1975 World Conference in Mexico City at which 125 nations took part at governmental level.

It is a mistake to write off 'international talking shops' as useless. What occurs in such gatherings, and the dissemination of records of their proceedings, does influence thinking and help to make a topic acceptable and even fashionable. The process of influencing world opinion is slow but progress is made. (Compare the growth of social approval of birth control, and of ecological, conservationist and antipollution programmes.)

An interesting development is the emergence of a supranational enforcement procedure for equal pay and equal opportunity within the EEC, based on Directives which bind the member states. This has already been used effectively by Belgian and Irish women. What is perhaps less generally known is that the more widely based Council of Europe has a monitoring procedure under its Social Charter which was ratified in 1965 and has Articles guaranteeing equal pay for work of equal value, twelve weeks paid maternity leave, and rights to vocational guidance and vocational training. The governments who subscribed to the Charter undertook to report on their domestic legislation every two years. While the Charter does not create legal rights for the individual, it does provide some leverage over governments through the supervisory mechanisms.[54]

The action of national governments in relation to equal opportunity has taken a number of forms, and has in some instances been linked with general endeavours to investigate and improve the status of women. One can distinguish five main types of agency or instrument. First, the creation of a post in government entitled 'Minister for the Status of Women'. This can be of cabinet rank or a junior ministerial post (France has tried both), or combined with another portfolio, as has happened in Canada. A variation of this is the appointment of a special adviser on women's affairs to the president or prime minister, of which the United States and Australia offer examples. These posts unfortunately tend to be more a public relations exercise than a genuine attempt to make significant changes. Their occupants are not given the sort of resources they would need to make a real impact. Finally, such posts can disappear overnight either at the whim of the politician who created them, or because he goes out of office. They may easily fall victim to conflicting political pressures, as when in 1978 the ministerial post in Iran was abolished as a sop to the religious-led opposition to the Shah.

Another device is to create a national council for the status of women to which members are appointed from women's organizations. These councils have quasi official status in that they are enabled to put their views direct to government. Like the special ministers or advisers, they are unlikely to be given significant resources and may receive none at all, as in the United Kingdom and, until recently, the Republic of Ireland. I noted in 1975[55] that the Federal Advisory Council on the Status of Women in Canada had a revenue of $476,000 and its salary bill was $210,000. I should estimate that this represents unusually generous provision for a body of this sort, though I should be happy to be proved wrong. (Canada allocated $5 million for International Women's Year projects. In the United Kingdom, it rated only £10,000.) There is a danger that such councils will reach only the lowest common denominator in their pronouncements, and that they will exclude the more radical elements of the women's movement. Both these pitfalls have been avoided in Ireland, where the Council for the Status of Women represents the full spectrum of women's groups and has, by patiently working together over a number of years, managed to reach a concensus at ever more progressive levels. Advisory Councils, like ministerial appointments, are generally the creatures of executive discretion and therefore have no guarantee of continuity. However the fact that they have identifiable constituencies behind them is some safeguard against arbitrary disbandment or downgrading.

The third type of agency is that exemplified by the Equal Opportunities Commission in the United States and Canadian and Australian commissions. These organizations have responsibility to make sure that equal employment opportunities are available to all, irrespective of race, colour, sex, religion or national origin. (The Ontario Human Rights Code adds 'age' and 'marital status' to the protected categories.) Thus the aim is to deal with all the major types of discrimination as part of general civil rights or human rights policy. In the USA, the black civil rights movement was mainly, if not solely, responsible for the passage of legislation. In Canada, a growing country with immigrants from many lands, a traditional French/English divide, and an indigenous population of Eskimos, it is clear that discrimination which inhibits the development or deployment of the talents of any citizen is both unjust and uneconomic. The Australian National Committee on Discrimination in Employment and Occupation was set up following Australia's ratification in 1973 of the ILO Convention No. 111 on Discrimination in Employment (1959).

A subspecies of the general agencies is the kind of commission established in Britain, Northern Ireland, the Republic of Ireland, Denmark, Sweden and some states of Australia, which is exclusively concerned with sex discrimination. It is a matter for debate, and no simple issue, whether it is more effective to cater separately for sex discrimination in this way. Much must depend on the circumstances of the individual country. Women are not a minority, and sex discrimination is practised equally by ethnic majorities and minorities. Women of minority ethnic origin tend usually to be at the bottom of the scale of pay and job opportunities. Will their position be more improved through a racial discrimination only agency, a sex discrimination only agency, or an agency with general anti-discriminatory powers? Whatever answer is adopted, the agencies will find that discriminatory techniques, and appropriate counter measures, have elements in common irrespective of who the victims are.

Both types of sex discrimination agency have usually been set up in association with legislation which makes sex discrimation illegal. Legislation is thus the fourth category of government instrument, and one which I shall examine in some detail below.

Finally, the fifth major type of government action is the use of government's own massive power as a purchaser of goods and services, and a funder of research, educational and health programmes to oblige commercial organizations and non-commercial institutions to develop policies for improving the opportunities of employed women. This has so far been attempted only in the United States. I shall return to the important subject of 'affirmative action' later.

These, then, are the principal ways in which governments have made a gesture, and sometimes more than a gesture, in the direction of establishing equality of the sexes in reality as well as in constitutional law. There is something distinctly anomalous about a governmental agency which is charged with promoting the interests of a group of citizens with full political rights who constitute half, or even a majority, of the population. Has the democratic process failed so notably that the majority has to be given special consideration? Or does the existence of these bodies constitute a recognition that political and legal rights have little or no impact on the fundamental inequalities between the sexes ? Perhaps it would be more accurate to say that the agencies are a practical, though inadequate, recognition of the fact that political and legal rights have been conceived in terms of male lifestyles and needs. When the British Member of Parliament, Helene Hayman, brought her baby into the House of Commons, she highlighted the reasons why the right to become a legislator under present conditions is one which many women feel they cannot exercise. A conscientious discharge of 'family responsibilities' is very difficult to combine with the duties of a legislator and is not in itself considered to qualify one for public office at a later stage. Since the normal channels have produced so very few women in legislatures, I think it would not be undemocratic to suggest that, in order to increase the representation of women in government, they should be brought in by methods other than that of direct election. This would be only an extension of the principle underlying the setting up of Status of Women Commissions and similar bodies. One of the most successful and popular ministers of our time, Madame Simone Weil, was appointed directly to the French Government and has never stood for election to the legislature. The same applies to many women life peers in the British House of Lords. Political scientists and students of government could consider other ways in which democracy could be adapted to equal male and female participation.

Meanwhile, the women and men who hold appointments as Ministers for the Feminine Condition, President's Special Advisers on Women's Affairs, and members of commissions of various kinds connected with women's interests, bear a far heavier representative responsibility than any individual elected legislator. This responsibility is all the more grave in that they are not always subject to normal democratic accountability.

Equal opportunity laws

As a first step towards assessing the adequacy, and thinking about future directions, of equal opportunity effort, I should like to examine the main features of some existing legislation. A full-scale comparative study is a research project I should like to recommend. Here I can only pick out some of the most important aspects.

Scope

The law may cover only direct, overt discrimination, but it is vital that indirect discrimination should also be included. Indirect discrimination occurs when requirements are imposed which appear on the surface to be sex neutral but which members of one sex find it more difficult to comply with than members of the other sex. Thus the British Civil Service Commission was held to be practising indirect discrimination by specifying an age band for applicants for certain junior posts. It was shown that fewer women than men could comply with these age limits because women job seekers tended to be returning to paid work after a break for child-rearing.[56] Other forms of indirect discrimination can involve physical requirements, such as height. A considerable case law has been built up in the United States.[57]

It is desirable also that the law should cover marital status as well as sex. The marriage bar is no longer with us, but it is not unknown for married women to be the first to be deprived of their jobs when lay-offs or redundancy occur. Married women are also discriminated against if they have young children, as employers fear that this will lead to absences from work, when a child is ill, for example. In South Australia and New South Wales coverage extends to people cohabiting otherwise than in marriage.[58]

Procedure for dealing with complaints

A crucial choice has to be made whether to funnel complaints through a central agency, with resort to the courts only if conciliation fails, or whether to allow, and leave, individuals or groups to pursue their own claims through the normal legal procedures or in specialized labour tribunals, where these exist. Centralizing complaints can lead to a backlog of cases building up, as has happened in the United States. On the other hand, if there is a direct resort to the courts, the agency may be left with little idea of what is happening in the field as a whole, claimants may miss out on much needed assistance with handling their cases, and the opportunity for building up a body of consistent practice and decisions may be lost. Labour courts and regular law courts may well have little expertise in dealing with sex discrimination, and are likely to be staffed entirely or predominantly by men. Unlike equal opportunity agencies, they have no commitment to promoting equal opportunity.

Decisions of the higher courts can, however, have an important effect on public opinion. They are bound to influence the behaviour of employers, who will not wish to fall foul of the equal opportunity law. The decision of a prestigious court is likely to carry considerably more weight than that of an informal labour tribunal, particularly since the latter is unlikely to constitute a precedent binding in other cases. Statements such as those made by Supreme Court judges that 'classifications based on sex . . . are inherently suspect and must therefore be subjected to strict judicial scrutiny' (Frontiero *v.* Richardson 1973), have an important opinion-forming function. In the past, the law enforced the sex stereotypes: all the more telling then when the highest judicial authority overthrows preconceptions about the roles of men and women. In Diaz *v.* Pan American (1971) a Federal circuit court ruled that it was discriminatory to insist that all airline flight attendants be female, and that alleged customer preference for stewardesses was not a relevant consideration. In Sprogis *v.* United Airlines Inc. (1971) a court struck down a company rule that air stewardesses had to be unmarried: such a rule had never been applied to male employees, and marital status was held to have no bearing on a woman's ability to carry out the job of stewardess. In Phillips *v.* Martin Marietta, also in 1971, the Supreme Court found that it was discriminatory to refuse to hire women with pre-school age children when men with children of that age were employed. Another cherished prejudice fell before the judicial axe when in 1972 it was ruled that sex was not relevant to the job of professional baseball umpire and the defendant, a professional baseball league, was ordered to revise its height and weight requirements, which operated to exclude women, and to set up new qualifications related to the requirements of the job.

An equally vital, and related, point is whether a class, or representative, action procedure is available in the courts. If a claim can be brought on behalf of a large number of people all suffering from the same discriminatory practice, the disadvantages of direct resort to law will be less: there will be funds to secure expert advice, lawyers will find it worthwhile to specialize in such cases, courts or tribunals will realize that more is at stake than in a case brought by a lone individual, and decisions will attract more publicity and have more weight, particularly if a large award of damages or back pay is made. The class action has proved a powerful weapon in the United States, and has been introduced into the New South Wales Act.

Another advantage of the class action is that it makes victimization much more difficult. In the United States, anonymity is guaranteed to anyone requesting an official investigation into an equal pay claim. Anything which reduces the pressure on individuals is to be welcomed. In civilized societies we surely no longer need to have martyrs before it can be established what fair treatment and good practice is?

Beyond the individual case

The question, whether it is up to *individuals* to work the law, to handle their own complaints and to bring suit so that precedents can be established, is central to the whole equal opportunity effort. In my view, the British legislation (to take one example) leans too far in this direction: there is no class action procedure and no central handling of complaints through the

Equal Opportunities Commission. While the individual must have legally enforceable rights, sporadic and unco-ordinated action by individuals will not bring about orderly changes on the desired scale. Legislation constitutes a statement that equal opportunity is national policy. This policy has to be implemented principally through the promulgation of codes of practice, wide-ranging investigations into whole companies or sectors of industry, and the formulation of comprehensive plans whose progress can be monitored. The most effective penalties against employers for failure to carry out equal opportunity policies are adverse publicity and substantial damages and other appropriate remedies awarded through a class action procedure. Any system that pins its faith on the action of single individuals will be ineffective. It is no light matter to take proceedings against an employing organization which can out-gun you in terms of expert advice and other resources. Many individuals will prefer to let the matter drop, and thus the development of the law through decided cases will be patchy.

Publicity

It is important that the law should be known and understood. The US Civil Rights Act 1964 called for one or more high level national conferences to be held to explain and publicize the law (Section 716). It also specifies that the provisions of the law shall be displayed in workplaces, trades union premises and employment agencies (Section 711). The Equal Employment Opportunities Commission has posters printed for use in complying with this section. That Commission has exercised much ingenuity in finding other means of publicity.[59]

The official agency

It is usual for the legislation to set up an agency which is responsible for promoting equal opportunity and overseeing the national effort. Italy is an exception in this respect. The agency may range from a single Commissioner to a numerous body. A significant factor is the provenance of the Commissioners and whether they are, or feel themselves to be, representative of some constituency. A particularly explicit example is the Republic of Ireland's Employment Equality Agency which statutorily must comprise two members representing employers and two representing workers and, of the remaining six members, three must represent women's organizations. (The latter are well integrated into official structures in Ireland.) Since employers and trades unions have been the major practisers of discrimination, there is a strong case against a constitution which enables them to form a bloc in the counsels of the agency. On the other hand, if they form powerful vested interests in the society at large, it may be difficult to exclude them. If this is so, such interests should certainly be balanced by feminist activists, and 'neutrals', and the Irish Act strives to achieve this. This is also the case in Denmark where women's representatives are in a majority (four) with three representatives of employers and unions, and a neutral President. Nevertheless, the constituency principle seems to me an erroneous one: the agency must be accountable to the community at large, since it is a public body using public funds. Its members should not have prior allegiances to those who nominated them. In the United States, the EEOC has only five members, appointed by the President without a constituency element. It has to account to a Congressional Committee for its performance. Some such mechanism is required and the publication of an annual report, though very desirable, is not a sufficient means of ensuring accountability.

The prime function of the equal opportunity agency is to undertake those aspects of implementing the equal opportunity policy which individuals or voluntary associations cannot, because they do not have the standing, power or resources. The agency should be able to talk to government and other official agencies on an equal footing, require them to take appropriate action and furnish information. Similarly, the agency should have, in relation to private sector employers, trade unions and employment agencies, powers which can reach the general policies and practices of such organizations, as distinct from their treatment of individual cases. Probably the most effective power of an agency is to conduct investigations, backed with enforcement powers if recommendations arising out of the investigation are not carried out. It was this combination of powers which enabled the EEOC to negotiate the consent decree for American Telephone and Telegraph whereby that corporation's personnel practices were changed significantly and made subject to regular monitoring. Not only did the EEOC score a great coup by bringing the country's biggest employer to book, but the compensation of $45 million awarded to AT&T employees on account of past discrimination made the rest of the corporate sector realize that equal opportunity for women was serious business.

Another important power is that of issuing Codes of Practice or Guidelines. While these do not have the same force as legislation, they can be highly influential, especially if they are approved by the law courts as statements of what good practice should be.

Specific duties of the agency may include the obligation to review other legislation with a view to eliminating sex discrimination. This obligation may be limited to 'protective' legislation as in the British and Irish Acts, or may range over all legislation, as in the State of Victoria. The New South Wales Anti-Discrimination Board is charged with examining not only all legislation but also government policies and practices and all superannuation funds and pension schemes.

Agencies have broad functions of promoting equal opportunity. The crucial question is whether there are adequate means of ensuring that these functions are vigorously discharged: is there provision in general administrative or constitutional law for requiring agencies to carry out the general duties assigned to them? (This is a separate question from political accountability.) In terms of the Common Law, for instance, does an action of mandamus lie against the agency if it is sluggardly? If it does, this is one way in which a group of individuals can involve itself in the general policy of the legislation, by applying to the Court for an order requiring the agency to perform specified functions.

Strategy for equal opportunity agencies

The lot of the official change agent is not a particularly easy one in that it is required to be exploratory and provocative within a bureaucratic framework. It may also be hampered by lack of resources, since its creation may be seen by government as a response to sectional political pressures which should be bought off as cheaply as possible.

The magnitude of the changes which the official agency is there to facilitate is such that substantial concrete achievement is liable to be long deferred. It is hardly conceivable that within the term of office of any present holder of an agency post there will have been a major shift in the sex-segregation of the work force. The task of the agency is to set the processes of change in motion and ensure that they will be irreversible. It can do this partly by institutionalizing change mechanisms and partly by nurturing the women's movement so that continuing political pressure is assured.

Change in the past has resulted from spasmodic campaigns and momentum has been lost because there were no institutions to carry through the pressure for continuous improvements. Thus, for example, when equal pay was obtained in the British Civil Service, the societies of women civil servants which had worked for this advance dissolved themselves. Women are, it seems, pathetically eager to believe that the latest gain represents the end of the battle for equality. It is unthinkable that it could have been suggested that, once the atom had been split, further research in nuclear physics was unnecessary: yet comparable full stops to co-ordinated effort have occurred over and over again in the women's movement.

The aim of the official change agency should be, therefore, to ensure its own perpetuation through attaining a constitu-

tional or legislative base, and to encourage the institutionalization and systematization of all possible means for effecting,
monitoring and perpetuating the desired changes in the
status of women. The deeper it can get its requirements embedded in corporate practice, in law and in bureaucratic procedures, the better. Routines that are written into computer
programmes and inscribed on the standing checklists of
legislatures, managers and administrators are not easy to
eradicate. If a removal or change is proposed, it should be
mandatory to hold a full and public debate on the question.
Such routines should be made proof against economy drives,
rationalization and covert annulment.

Instead of moving from one limited goal to another, the
agencies and the women's movement should create a national
agenda, regularly reviewed, which sets out all the objectives.
Such an agenda will not only dispel any illusion that equality
has arrived because one specific measure has been achieved; it
can also serve as a tool for monitoring progress and setbacks.

The agencies need to see to it that women, the actual and
potential beneficiaries of this effort, understand what is being
done and appreciate the need for long term programmes and
built-in systems. One of the most potent ways of doing this
will be to teach, to both sexes, the history of the women's
movement and of its achievements and setbacks, so that each
new generation does not need to start from the beginning, to
re-invent the wheel of feminist consciousness. Publicity and
education should continually draw attention to the goals still
to be met.

Another essential strategy is to encourage the women's
movement and to give it status in the community. Activists
should be included among the members of the agency, as in
Ireland, and recruited to official working parties and committees. Women's groups should be helped with grants and
administrative back-up to carry out projects relevant to the
work of the agencies. Privileges such as favourable tax status
and official recognition should be withdrawn from women's
organizations which purport to be representative of women's
interests but which do not include women's rights work in

their regular programmes. The agency members and staff should have regular direct contact with activists as a mutual reinforcement and information sharing exercise. Dilution of the efforts and enthusiasm of agencies is likely to occur through the sheer psychological fatigue of continual engagement with those opposed to their aim, or at any rate apathetic. Agencies have a primary duty to keep up their own morale and that of their staff and supporting organizations outside.

How conciliatory should an EO agency be towards interests opposed to it? Agencies are exposed to temptations in that they have to negotiate with men who want to do as little as possible to implement equal opportunity and may be highly resistant to affirmative action. In addition, agencies may, in the cause of appealing to the decent feelings of reasonable people for support, disown basic feminist attitudes because they think that such attitudes will not appeal to the majority. The result, in terms of the public stance of the agency, will look perilously like that of the traditionally powerless woman who gets her way by wiles and subterfuge.

The agency should be unshakeable in its principles and make it clear that it is aiming for the highest level of implementation in the shortest possible timespan. The primary object of the agency is to change people's behaviour, not their opinions. (This principle is firmly embedded in the United States' system.) Nonetheless, the agency should never disown, or cast doubt on the justice of, the feminist cause. To do so would be equivalent to an admission by members of a racial equality commission that they could see that there was a case to be made for racial discrimination. Such pejorative statements have a damaging effect on the morale of the women's movement and do nothing to enhance the agency's standing with the uncommitted. They can only hearten those who are already opposed to the women's movement since the suggestion will be that the agency is vulnerable to taunts about the 'ridiculous' nature of 'extremist' feminist positions, and will therefore tend to draw back and moderate its requirements for practical measures if attacked on these lines.

Affirmative action

Affirmative action is a principle created under the United States' equal employment opportunity policy. It states that it is not sufficient to stop discriminating from now on, but that in addition steps must be taken to put right the effects of past discrimination. The main legal instrument by means of which this policy is given effect is the Presidential Executive Order, and the leverage is supplied by the government's purchasing policy. Under a series of Orders, beginning with No. 11246 of 1965, all government contractors (which means virtually all firms of any significance) have been under a duty to create an affirmative action programme. This requirement has been elaborated over the years and the so-called 'Revised Order 4' of 1972 (as amended) sets out in very considerable detail the action that is to be taken. Section 2.10 of the Order sums up the approach: 'An affirmative action program is a set of specific and result-oriented procedures to which a contractor commits himself to apply every good faith effort. . . . Procedures without effort to make them work are meaningless; and effort, undirected by specific and meaningful procedures, is inadequate.' The next sentence introduces two key concepts: 'An acceptable affirmative action program must include an *analysis* of areas within which the contractor is deficient in the utilisation of minority groups and women, and further, *goals and timetables* to which the contractor's good faith efforts must be directed to correct the deficiencies and thus to achieve prompt and full utilization of minorities and women, at all levels and in all segments of his workforce where deficiencies exist.' (Stress added.) Revised Order 14 details the procedures by which compliance is to be audited by the enforcing agency – these include both a 'desk audit' and a review to be carried out at the firm's premises. In addition, firms have to make regular returns on the composition of their workforce.

An important feature of the Executive Order system is that the affirmative action programme has to be undertaken irrespective of whether there has been any complaint under the legislation. The system therefore obviates the deficiencies and unpleasantness which characterize the investigation of individual complaints. The procedure is not accusatory but positively 'result-oriented'. The baseline is provided by a systematic analysis of the workforce at all levels.

There has been disagreement about the legality and efficacy of the 'goals and timetables' approach. It has particularly been a matter for hot dispute in the university world, where both the methods for appointing people to the coveted tenured posts and the criteria for judging between candidates are not as susceptible to the affirmative action process as those used in business.

Looking to the wider employment scene, it is clear that affirmative action does not mean giving jobs to unqualified women in accordance with an arbitrary quota system. Title VII of the Civil Rights Act states that there is no legal requirement to give preferential treatment to members of the protected groups, and Revised Order 4 says that, 'No contractor's compliance status shall be judged alone by whether or not he reaches his goals and meets his timetables' (para. 2.14). It can also be pointed out that it is not in the interests of the proponents of equal opportunity to thrust women into posts for which they are not qualified: their failure on the job would discredit the policy, and their personal anguish at failing would be a powerful form of negative public relations, depressing the aspirations of other women. However, in view of the basic premise that the level of utilization of women (or minority group members) in an organization should approximate to the proposition of qualified people in the category in the available pool of labour, numerical targets and timetables are essential to ensure that the required level of utilization comes about within a reasonable time. After some years' experience of the equal opportunity effort, employers are prepared to concede that it has improved their use of human resources generally. Mr G. E. Kofke of American Telephone and Telegraph has said that benefits of the affirmative action in that company include 'Better (more systematic) use of our entire talent pool' and 'improvements in selection, training, appraisals and career planning'.[60]

The problems of educational disadvantage require special treatment and are beyond the scope of this work but it should be noted that discrimination in education has also received legislative attention in the United States and in the British Sex Discrimination Act. It is axiomatic that equal employment opportunity must be underpinned by the educational system, so that people entering the labour market are equipped to take up the new opportunities open to them. As long as schools steer girls into arts 'options', cooking, housecraft, typing and biology, and away from maths, 'hard science', technical drawing and craft work, they will emerge unqualified to reap the benefits of any sex discrimination law in an industrial nation.

This sketch can give only an outline of the unique efforts being made in the United States, and the reader is referred to the specialist literature cited in the bibliography for the details. Modest results are showing up in the statistics, as Shaeffer and Axel's Chartbook shows. These results can be expected to improve as the affirmative action programmes continue: they have not been geared to achieving results overnight. To take just one example, the Bank of California undertook in 1974 goals under which, by the end of 1982, women would hold 35% of middle-management and 16% of senior management jobs; the Bank also set up a fund to provide complementary staff training and development.

These goals were established, like those of American Telephone and Telegraph, under a consent decree: but the courts have power to order affirmative action in a case where discriminatory practice has been found to exist. (Civil Rights Act 1964, s. 706 as amended: and see Rios *v.* Enterprise Association Steamfitters Local 638 of UA 501 F 2d. 622 (1974) a decision of the US Court of Appeals Second Circuit (New York)).[61] Similarly explicit powers do not appear in the legislation of other countries that I have examined.[62] Yet if the social evil of sex discrimination is to be eliminated, the limitation of legal remedies to dealing with individual cases of past discrimination (rather than changing employment practice for the future) must be abandoned.

While there are no comprehensive national programmes in Europe, some schemes have been devised to assist the entry of women into non-traditional occupations. In 1973, on an initiative of the Prime Minister's Advisory Council on Equality, Sweden began a pilot scheme in Kristianstad county, where there was high unemployment among women while at the same time some industries were experiencing shortages of manpower. A number of firms agreed to try out women in 'male' jobs such as lathe operators, painters, electricians, drillers and milling machine operators. Careful steps were then taken to inform women of what was proposed, and women who volunteered to take part in the scheme were given a three-week general induction and orientation course before beginning work. Fourteen companies took part and 123 women were given jobs. A detailed assessment of the scheme (Liljeström and others op. cit.) fairly sets out the successes and the difficulties. Similar schemes were started in five other counties in April 1975.

Special grants to employers who train girls and women for non-traditional occupations have been instituted in Sweden and in North Rhine Westphalia. The Swedish scheme also applies where males are trained for traditional 'women's work'. Germany also offers examples of government supported pilot schemes for training females for 'men's work'.[63] In Britain, the Engineering Industry Training Board has a scheme for scholarships to enable girls to become technicians. In France, a national scheme was launched in the autumn of 1978 to help women obtain industrial training. The two objectives of this are to reduce unemployment among women and to encourage them to try work which is outside the narrow range usually considered by, and offered to, women. Among these rather sparse examples of affirmative action, the programme running at Ashridge Management College, England, deserves a mention. Twelve major employing organizations are co-operating in a two to three year study of barriers to women's becoming managers and, more important, techniques for overcoming these difficulties. It is intended that there shall be a practical outcome in the increase in numbers of women in managerial positions. The project is being officially funded through the Training Services Agency. It is to be hoped that confidentiality will not impede a full publication of the results of this venture.

Finally, the Danish equal opportunity law provides for the Minister to grant exemptions in particular cases where this would promote equal opportunities. (Normally exemption provisions allow the continuance of sex discrimination.) It will be interesting to see what use is made of this power to authorize affirmative action.

6 EQUAL OPPORTUNITY - IN 2080?

'The Statesman who falls is he who does much,
and thus injures many.
The Statesman who stands the longest is he who
does nothing and injures no-one.'

> Anthony Trollope
> *The Duke's Children*, 1880
> (Chapter XXI)

'A knowledge of, and a reverence for, the
principles for which we have striven ought to
be kept alive, for these principles are very far
from being yet so clearly recognised as that
our children and our children's children may not
be called upon to rise again and again in their
defence.'

> Josephine Butler
> 'Personal Reminiscences of a Great Crusade'
> 1898

Speeding up the pace of change

We are constantly being told that people in modern, highly
developed countries are reeling, punch-drunk with the pace
of change. This cannot be said to apply to progress for
women. It has taken two centuries for women to gain political rights – at the beginning of the 1970s there were women
in Europe who still did not have the vote. Equal pay legis-

lation took about eighty years to achieve, and is still far from fulfilment in terms of equal pay as an economic reality. Equal pay depends on equal opportunity – how long will it be before we have it? Are the present measures sufficient to bring it about?

The evidence is abundant that the removal of formal barriers to women's entering occupations previously reserved for men is not enough to bring about equal opportunity in practice. We know that women are capable of doing professional, managerial and skilled craft jobs, but very few are realizing their potential. Even where there is a long-standing equal opportunity policy, as in the kibbutzim and in the teaching profession, women are still found in traditional 'women's work', servicing men and small children, and few women appear in the more senior ranks and the prestigious appointments. In professions created by women, such as personnel work, social work and nursing, men now have a high proportion of the senior posts.

It is clear that positive action is needed if women are to exercise their talents and skills in work for which they are fitted. The complementary principle is that society is deliberately impoverishing itself by neglecting and under-utilizing women's abilities.

In the United States, the action is mildly coercive, through the affirmative action policy backed by the power the federal government can wield as a massive purchaser of goods and services and a funder of education and research. The legislation gives the Equal Employment Opportunities Commission, and groups of employees, the power, through the courts, to call great corporations to account and to secure damages and back pay awards so large that equal opportunity and affirmative action secure a place at the top of corporate agendas. Despite some protest about the unreasonableness of the authorities, and criticism of the administrative arrangements, the policies are firmly entrenched and are working. They are even admitted to have had a beneficial effect on personnel practice. All this has been achieved since 1964, or on an alternative view of the history, since 1972, when the

EEOC's powers were strengthened and it began to use some real muscle on sex discrimination.

Other governments have tended to take the view epitomized by my quotation from Trollope. Policies designed to improve the status of women in employment are primarily seen as a threat to the vested interests of men. Equal opportunity for women must mean, it is feared, fewer opportunities for men. Men will not like competition from women. Governments to whom free competition between enterprises is an article of faith, blanch at the thought of free competition between men and women in the labour force. Yet the underlying principle is the same – the nation loses if assets, human or material, are not used efficiently.

The efforts at affirmative action in European countries, of which I gave examples in Chapter 5, are of a somewhat tentative nature. They eschew the stick and offer the carrot instead. Equal opportunity is given a 'soft sell' No doubt this approach is influenced by the presence of a recession – the United States began its affirmative action in an expansionary period, before the oil crisis – but the precedent is an ominous one.

One of the most effective pressure groups in the States, WEAL (Women's Equity Action League), had a question on its recruiting literature at one time – 'Tired of feminist rhetoric?' In Europe, we have had a great many official reports full of rhetoric about women's employment problems. Instead of qualitative statements, we should have quantitative plans for the labour market, and for education and training, to break up the female labour ghettoes within a given time scale. Even if the time scale is very long, the plans must be made and action started at once.

In Chapter 1, I said that women cannot make their own creative and spontaneous contribution if they are isolated and feel themselves to be constantly under scrutiny. We still have too many reports in the press about women who are the 'first' and only – holder of heavy goods vehicle licence, electrician, bricklayer. These women are still made to feel that they are freaks – both through the hostility of their male counterparts[64] and through the patronizing attitudes and false glamourizing of the media. We must think instead of the first twenty, the first fifty, in apprenticeships, management traineeships and promotion to previously male-only levels of responsibility within a single firm. This will mean the end of pussy-footing with equal opportunity and instead putting it on a basis of professionalism in terms of targets, methods and management responsibility. It seems very unlikely to me that this will come about without some measure of compulsion in the form of a government-backed national policy with rewards and penalties. It is changes in behaviour which count, not changes in attitudes. We could wait another half century for attitudes to budge, particularly as attitudes in parts of industry seem to be behind those in the population as a whole.[65] If employing organizations had declared and well-publicized equal opportunity policies, with the authority of top management behind them, and with a guarantee that necessary training and other support would be made available, I think we should hear a great deal less about 'women not wanting to take the responsibility' of a job at the next level. If women know that company policy (i.e. the male hierarchy) is based on women progressing naturally, as men do, that the organization expects them to move on rather than stick at some level which the women's washroom has sensed is 'the highest a woman can ever get here', then they will respond. At present, women who move on lose the cameraderie of 'the girls' without becoming 'one of the boys'.

Equal representation, not just equal opportunity

We know that there are many women who feel that they are under-used. This is, for instance, a well-known characteristic of personal secretaries, who sometimes take the extra responsibility, providing expert support to an executive, but not receiving an assistant manager's salary. Gradualism in implementing equal opportunity is for the benefit of men, not women.

Since women form 40% or more of the labour force, and this percentage is growing, the affirmative action will have to operate fast to close the gap between that figure and the low percentage of women in skilled, technical, professional and executive posts in both public and private sectors.

This declaration of a policy of 'proportional representation' on my part will no doubt raise a few eyebrows. Let me explain why it is necessary and possible, and dispose of some objections.

To go back to first principles: there are several arguments for throwing all jobs open to both sexes. First, that there are very few jobs that are uniquely suited to one sex only. (Wet nurse is a rare example of a job which members of the male sex are physically unable to perform). Assumptions that no man, or no woman, will have a characteristic objectively identified as essential for performing a particular job are usually unjustified. Second, in a society where the possession of a job is essential to economic viability and status, it is unjust to debar people from access to jobs on the grounds of sex alone. Third, sex discrimination is incompatible with democratic principles which dictate that all citizens shall have the same rights and opportunities. Fourth, it is wasteful to neglect the talents of half the population.

However, as we have seen, the right of access to qualifications and to occupations does not lead necessarily to a take-up of the opportunities. Social justice is not satisfied by providing 'equal opportunities' which remain a dead letter for all but a few exceptionally highly-motivated people. An American professor of medicine, Estelle Ramey, once said, 'Equality is not when a female Einstein gets promoted to Assistant Professor; equality is when a female schlemiel moves ahead as fast as a male schlemiel.'[66]

Women have the ability to make 40% of the middle and top jobs instead of being crowded into the lowest strata: so they should be up there, using their talents and, equally important, redressing the balance on behalf of all women in their decision-making and planning for the future. Thus the argument for sex balance in organizations is that due regard should be paid in the ordering of work and in personnel policies to the differences between the life-styles and needs of the sexes: if one sex dominates it will use its power and influence in its own favour and ignore or neglect the situation of the other sex. Just as women, having to obey the laws and pay taxes, should be equally represented in government, so they should wield a proportionate influence in the 'government' of their workplace and the organization which employs them.

This argument applies not only to management but also to trade union representation and to worker participation and industrial democracy: and in these latter instances it is arguable that there ought to be quotas at the start, so that women get proportional representation on works councils, supervisory boards and the rest of the apparatus of power-sharing in employment.

Objections to programme for equal representation soon

The objects that will be raised to this programme for rapid progress to real sex parity in employment are first, women are not qualified to move into 'senior' jobs (forewoman to chief executive and everything in between); second, women don't want extra responsibility; and third, 'what about the children?'

On qualifications, the first step in any affirmative action programme is an audit of the qualifications already possessed by women staff. The results of this may surprise some employers. Next, are the qualifications demanded by the employer really necessary? (There is a useful body of American case law on this.) If they are necessary, arrange for the women to have the training, so they can get the qualification just as men do; and on the same terms, not paying to put themselves through night school while men have time off on full pay during the day, with tuition fees paid by the company.

The next hurdle that will be raised is 'experience'. Paper qualification there can be no arguing about, but the demand for 'the right type of experience' is a classic tool of discrimination. Make sure someone never gets that experience, and that person will never rise. Women's lack of experience is, of course, one of the results of discrimination in the past. Is experience irreplaceable?

In the days before knowledge was generally available in books, the old man or woman who could remember an unusual state of affairs, such as chronic drought, who had 'seen it all before', did have a value to the community which younger people did not. They could remember what had been done about the crisis, they could reassure people that you could live through such a period. They could recall the judgements and sayings of past leaders and wiseacres. They would have known present leaders, and most other members of the community, all their lives.

Nowadays people do not have that kind of experience, unique to themselves, particularly in industry, with its constant innovation. Through education, and reading on our own, we can obtain the benefit of the thoughts and experience of hundreds of people we shall never meet, tested against all kinds of conditions.

'Experience' can be claimed as a compensation by those who have not had the chance of an education, or of training, to defend themselves against those with 'book-learning'. It can be the consolation of the middle-aged, or their weapon, in the face of upstart youngsters, who seem to 'know it all'. It can be invoked as a reason for promoting men who have been with the firm for a long time, a reward for loyalty. Defined subjectively, it can be a pretext for keeping out people you would prefer not to have inside. It is also a standard excuse for giving the top jobs to people nearing retirement.

Clearly, experience in a job can improve performance, but not in a linear progression into infinity. On the contrary, performance may decline if the person becomes bored, stale or discontented; and there are very few, if any, jobs where continuous improvement is possible.

Experience can be required in the sense of having carried

out a number of different roles in the organization. Bankers are supposed to work their way up from being cashiers, so they have seen all sides of the business. Sales experience is sometimes considered essential. Inspectors on buses may be required to have had experience as bus drivers.[67] It is questionable how much of this kind of experience is strictly necessary and, as with qualifications, its relevance to the job for which any particular person is being considered should be rigorously examined. If it is found to be genuinely necessary, then women must be given the opportunity to acquire it, as men do.

This brings us to the question of breaks for having a baby or looking after small children. While men are acquiring 'valuable experience', women are dulling their minds by month after month of almost ceaseless exposure to the demands and the concentration-destroying cries or chatter of babies and toddlers. At worst, years of this can result in a woman's needing a refresher course in being a mentally active human being: the kind of course that is offered by the institute in Paris set up by the writer and researcher, Evelyn Sullerot. At best, the young mother may have organized her life so that she keeps up with her professional expertise and contacts and takes on part-time employment to keep her hand in. She may be able to work from home, either freelance, or through an employment agency which specializes in her kind of need. The children reach the age when they go to school or kindergarten all day. The mother applies for full-time work in the kind of business where she worked previously and for which she is trained. She is likely to be told that she must make up the missing 'experience' and cannot expect to compete on equal terms with her male contemporaries, or with women who have had no break. I suspect this is often just a way of saying that those who have given continuous service to the organization will be extremely disgruntled if married women returners are given credit in seniority terms for the child-rearing years. It seems peculiarly cruel of society to encourage young women to give up paid employment when their children are small and then, instead of rewarding them for this allegedly socially beneficial sacrifice, to penalize them for the rest of their working lives.

There is a case for taking home management experience as a proxy for experience in paid employment, since it involves budgeting and careful scheduling of timetables and of use of resources such as the family car, the deep freeze, and so on. More needs to be done to enable women to recognize this experience as relevant to outside management jobs and to present it in terms that translate into the language of personnel managers. The same applies to voluntary work which can provide experience of fund-raising and finance, marketing, public relations, team management and use and development of human resources.

If, in the last analysis, it is found that there is some experience which the returner really must have, then it should be provided in as concentrated form as possible and supplemented by training. If it is declared company policy that this will be done, to accelerate the re-integration of returners, and if in addition there is a national policy backing the firm's action, complaints of unfairness can be more easily met. If men are facing competition they did not have before, they will also have the satisfaction of knowing that their own wives can reap the benefit of the system too. If the child-rearing break is institutionalized in this way, it should of course be open to either parent. We can see the beginnings of this in paternity leave and in the Swedish entitlement for either parent to take a child-rearing leave of absence for seven months after the birth, receiving a parenthood allowance from the state which amounts to about 90% of normal pay.

I have already dealt with the thesis that women don't want more demanding jobs, and suggested that it is the environment rather than the job which deters some women. There is the added factor that more responsibility at work does not mean less responsibility at home. The more senior job is likely to trench on both the time and the mental and physical energy at present devoted to domestic tasks. Women may also be worried about the effect on marital relations of their being paid more than, or outranking, their husbands. A vigorous affirmative action plan implies the re-negotiation of the roles within marriage, but this is happening already. Education and counselling can help with the adjustment, and television plays and soap operas (and advertisements) could explore the theme and familiarize people with the complexities, rather than endlessly reinforcing the outworn stereotypes.

Last, the children, a subject which merits a book on its own. I hope I shall not be accused of being a child-hater if I describe children as the final fetter. It is important to remind ourselves that the idea of children as a leisured section of the community, attending full-time education and debarred by law from taking up paid employment, is entirely modern. Until the last century children were set to work as soon as they were capable of doing something useful.[68] Since in law the father was the sole guardian of the children, many men were minor entrepreneurs or employers in the sense that they had an absolute right to dispose of the labour of their children. As children ceased to be a source of income and became instead a responsibility, maintained by their parents until school-leaving age (which was raised a number of times), father's rights became of little value and gradually mother's rights to guardianship and custody evolved. On divorce, children were almost automatically given into the mother's care, whether she was the 'innocent' or 'guilty' party. The mother-child relationship became idealized.[69] Motherhood could even be called a vocation.

However, while there was much concern about the physical welfare of children of working-class mothers taking jobs outside the home, a concern which was still manifesting itself in the 1950s and 1960s in the debate on whether married women should go out to work, the practice in middle and upper-class families of employing nannies and nursery-maids to look after the children was considered normal and proper. There was no suggestion of ill effects on the children's development and 'nanny' was often a much-loved member of the family circle.

During the Second World War, women from the middle classes moved into employment. (In Britain, women were liable to the direction of labour regulations unless they had young children.) Already they had the legal right to enter most occupations, and having had a taste of outside work and their own salary during the war, it could have been predicted that a lot of them might decide to stay in paid employment.

Many women had blazed trails in the inter-war period, pioneering women's entry into a wide variety of jobs. Now, in the period of post-war reconstruction, would be the time for the follow-through. However, the male middle-class professionals came up with an answer to this – 'maternal deprivation'. No longer was it respectable to use nannies. A child needed a mystical bond with one person (the mother, of course!) for the first several years. Any attempt to share care of the infant with helpers would have serious effects on development. Thus mothers were saddled with endless guilt and anxiety. Nothing could be more selfish than sacrificing the child's psychic stability to a mere career. On the other hand, if the mother was nonetheless bold enough to hand the child to a 'mother-substitute', she was threatened with becoming a complete stranger to her offspring, her place having been usurped by the nurse. The authors of 'Women and Medicine' point out that this myth has survived many telling attacks, and attribute this to its massive social convenience. For instance, it has been used as an excuse by central and local government for not providing child care facilities.[70] It is also, of course, a splendid way of keeping able young women out of the competition for the better white-collar jobs. One surmises that one reason for the fall in the birth-rate is a silent female revolt against being fettered by this emotional blackmail.

Children are the joint and equal responsibility of parents; and society in general has an interest in ensuring that the rising generation is healthy, well-adjusted and adequately educated. We must end the pretence that women have exclusive responsibility for children. We can also question the assumption that women are 'naturally' better at caring for them. After all, very few men have been tried out in this role so far. Saying 'I wouldn't be any good at it' is sometimes a rationalization of 'I don't want to do it'. On the other hand, men who do want to share child care should be encouraged and helped, and not fended off by female monopolists, provided they are prepared to share the messy and unpleasant side of the job and do not pick out only the elements which give job satisfaction and pleasure.

A core for the movement: institutions of learning

My second quotation, from Josephine Butler, is another reminder that the future of the women's movement must be sustained through an appreciation of its past. How many women today know who Josephine Butler was, or have heard of the national and international campaigns which she inspired? Yet the issues she tackled so heroically – the licensing and compulsory medical examination of prostittutes, in the interests of male customers subject to no legal restrictions themselves – are as vital today as ever they were. There are still suggestions that married women should give up their jobs in favour of men when there is unemployment. The faults of young people are blamed on mothers in paid employment. We must all be made aware of the threats to what has been gained if we are not to fight the old campaigns over and over again. This means educating young people, of both sexes, in the history of women's political rights and women's employment in the same way as they now learn the history of men's political and social evolution. 'Women's studies' in universities and other branches of higher and further education should not be looked on as an ephemeral phenomenon which can be dispensed with once it has made its point. It is ironic that there has been so much pressure to make women's colleges into unisex institutions in the very era when there was never more need for women to have their own place in the world of scholarship and the right atmosphere for developing the exciting ideas of the new women's movement. (This dilemma was, however, appreciated and debated by the students and alumnae of Radcliffe in connection with the proposal for fusion with Harvard.[71])

As long as co-educational institutions operate discriminatory practices, there is need for centres of excellence for girls and women where their needs will be given the same consideration and as good resources as men and boys have in mixed schools and colleges. Of course all girls should have as good an education as boys, but it is not possible to reverse the co-educational situation completely and to do so now would not guarantee equality; but let us at least keep such institutions for girls and women as we have, and use them as the intellectual power houses of feminism, instead of flinging them away under the influence of our persistent delusion that 'full equality has now been achieved'. When it has indeed been achieved, such places will decline of their own accord; they will not have to be planned, or legislated, out of existence.

It is yet another delusion to think that the younger generation will not repeat the old patterns of sex discrimination, and can be safely left to bring in the new era of equal opportunities. Some young people are indeed behaving and thinking differently, but attitudes to the roles of men and women are not neatly aligned along the generation gap. At the time I was completing this book, I met a young man at a business dinner; he was employed by a large management training organization. He announced that his wife was going to stay at home until their youngest child was sixteen years old. In the group was a white-haired executive from a well-known manfacturing company who had just been telling me about the number of women workers in his company who had completed thirty or more years of continuous service despite their family responsibilities. He laughed at the young man's assurance.

Final reflections

This book has offered some ideas about work and our attitudes to it. I hope that readers will take away some of these ideas and will find them useful, whether or not they agree with my major theses. The world of paid employment is changing rapidly and there is plenty of scope, and need, for creative thinking about all aspects of it. Unpaid work is undergoing much change too. The growth of pressure groups and interest groups of all kinds outside the formal structures of party politics, organized and staffed by volunteers, has become a major feature of public life, for example. Do-it-yourself activities in the home have also become an important part of life for many people. At many levels people see the need to get things done, but the regular structure of paid employment, whether of politicians or painters, is not accomplishing these things. Instead people are using their positions in paid employment, or in the home, as a base supporting all sorts of other activities which certainly qualify as 'work' in my definition but which are not paid or given official recognition as a legitimate part of the social fabric. Thus the points that I have made about the omission of many worthwhile, and essential, activities from what society recognizes as 'work' do not relate only to the activities of women.

Was it correct for Engels and his followers to think in terms of enabling women to share in the dignity of productive labour, or was that another male-biased, though well-intentioned notion? Is productive work intrinsically better than service work, or was it given greater esteem by a male-dominated society because it was the kind of work that men did? Nowadays we see the number of people employed in productive work, that is, in agriculture and manufacturing, decreasing continuously. The industrial robot and the automated factor are already a reality. Mature economies are characterized by an increase in service functions, including education and medical services.

However, the most brilliant technology will not in itself provide a solution to the sex segregation of the labour market. In fact, it may well exacerbate it, since so few scientists and technologists are women. How many of those planning the industrial investment for the next ten or twenty years, the research and development programmes which will shape so much of our future, are women? How many of the futurologists and science fiction writers who give us scenarios of the decades ahead of us? Women are understandably sceptical about the benefits of space exploration and ever higher technology. Will it take a third world war before men admit (if any of them survive) that their continual urge to escape from human relations into mechanical things and abstractions, to explore the unknown before the known was properly understood, and to resort to violence so readily has been a little misguided?

Women may not be so well-qualified as many men in science and technology, in capital investment appraisal, or in the techniques of inflicting torture and mega-death: but they are fully qualified human beings, and maybe better integrated than men, who have sacrificed themselves to super specilization and the gods of the organization, whether it be a company or a nation state

Perhaps one day we shall be able to operate the world in a mode which leaves behind the whole concept of human beings having power over other human beings. Meanwhile, to suggest, as I have done, that women, who are in the majority, should now occupy four out of every ten decision-making positions, constitutes a very modest proposal.

NOTES AND REFERENCES

Anatomy of a Feminist – a personal foreword

[1] One of the members of the British House of Lords Select Committee on the Anti-Discrimination Bill 1972–73, a highly distinguished man who had spent a lifetime in legal practice, expressed amazement at the amount of discrimination against women which was revealed in evidence to the Committee.

[2] 1919 was the year in which the profession was opened to women under the Sex Disqualification (Removal) Act.

[3] See Hennig and Jardim, *The Managerial Woman*, pp. 5ff. The authors' survey of women middle managers carried out from Harvard Business School in 1973 showed that a decision to shape the career in a purposeful way was invariably made at the age of thirty to thirty-three, after ten years or more of continuous employment.

[4] I am not sure whether this would be acknowledged by all as a specifically Christian principle but I identify it with my Christian education.

[5] So do millions of others, judging by the Marian cult, and devotion to Kuan Yu, goddess of mercy.

[6] It is worth noting that neither the club nor the client company could have been called to account under the Sex Discrimination Act if it had been in force at the time. It is interesting to speculate whether an industrial tribunal would have found my employers guilty of discrimination in excluding me from a fringe benefit!

Chapter 1

[7] See Oakley, pp. 92–95. Her survey found that the housewife's working week ranged from forty to over a hundred hours. Most

worked over seventy hours a week. This compares with the forty hours standard in industry.

8 This view is epitomized by the slogan coined in the women's movement in the USA – 'Housework is shitwork'.

9 Olive Schreiner, *Women and Labour*, 1911, reprinted by Virago Limited, 1978, p. 40.

10 See *Women and Medicine* by Joyce Leeson and Judith Gray, Tavistock, 1978, pp. 52–54.

11 My grandmother, as a child in the 1890s, had to undertake, as one of her regular good works, visits to a household of three sisters, one of whom was insane. She would take tea with the two normal ladies, terrified by the noises off, and by the occasional appearances of the poor mad sister. One can imagine what a terrible burden the care of this sister was to the other two.

12 These factors do not provide a complete explanation. For instance, they do not account for the fact that religious women, vowed to celibacy, were not permitted to enter the priesthood.

13 Infant mortality among the children of women factory workers was ascribed to the long absences of the mother from home and the inadequacy of substitutes; in particular infant mortality (and morbidity) were put down to the inability of factory workers to breastfeed their babies. See for example, *Women in Industry from Seven Points of View*, by G. M. Tuckwell and others (1908).

14 The uneasy application of 'modern management techniques' to nursing at ward level is documented in *A study of hospital management training in its organizational context* by Julia Davies, Manchester Business School, 1972.

15 A producer of television documentaries once told me that, on a visit to an old factory in Britain, he had been shown a door with a round hole in it. Through this hole the working mother had proferred her breast while her child was held up by the childminder on the other side of the door.

16 The proceedings of this seminar are recorded in *Women and the Scientific Professions*, edited by Mattfeld and Van Aken, MIT Press, 1965.

17 A result of this may be more effective pressure for provision of child facilities. One reason these tend to be in short supply, particularly in Britain, is that there is little middle class demand for them.

[18] An illustration of this is the British Civil Service where there has been equal pay and equal opportunity for nearly twenty years – yet women comprise less than 8% of those in the posts from Senior Executive Officer to Permanent Secretary. (Civil Service Statistics, 1978, HMSO.)

[19] My account of the history of personnel management is drawn from Mary Niven's excellent book, *Personnel Management 1913–1963*, IPM, 1967.

[20] p. 80, ibid.

[21] p. 125, ibid.

[22] HL 160, Session 1971–72, p. 161.

[23] Some of these are reviewed in Stead's article listed in the bibliography.

[24] The Writings of the Gilbreths, ed. Spriegel and Myers, Richard D. Irwin, 1953.

Chapter 2

[25] F. Engels, The origin of the family, quoted in Rowbotham, op. cit.

[26] Mitchell, op. cit., pp. 84ff.; and see the essay 'The Grand Coolie Damn' and statement on Birth Control by a black women's liberation group in *Sisterhood is Powerful*, ed. Robin Morgan, Vintage Books, New York, 1970.

[27] *Economics and the Public Purpose*, J. K. Galbraith, André Deutsch, 1974, p. 33.

[28] Turnbull and Williams' study – details in bibliography.

[29] Kahne and Kohen, op. cit., in bibliography, p. 1258.

[30] *Sex Discrimination in the Labour Market*, Brian Chiplin and Peter J. Sloane, Macmillan, 1976.

[31] Ghez and Becker, op. cit., p. 101.

[32] Pigou, op. cit., p. 566.

[33] Oakley, op. cit., pp. 19ff.

[34] R. Blauner, *Alienation and Freedom*, University of Chicago Press, 1964.

[35] One of the most blatant examples of this split between professed views and conduct is Rousseau, the apostle of sensibility and of enlightened upbringing of children. He consigned all five

of his own infant children by his faithful mistress to the Foundling Hospital in Paris and never saw them again. Perhaps his mature opinions were a form of expiation, like Meredith's novels, which championed the cause of women, after his own oppressive behaviour to his wife and her death only twelve years after their marriage. Rousseau, however, envisaged a circumscribed, submissive and passive role for women – see the critique in Eva Figes' book *Patriarchal Attitudes*.

36 Have women in fact ever worked for 'pin money'? It would be interesting to know the origins of this phrase which crops up even today, when the uses of 'pins' (an idle luxury?) are long forgotten.

37 'Labour Turnover', Occasional Paper No. 1, Dec. 1967, EDC for the Clothing Industry National Economic Development Office. This paper issued from the deliberations of a working party, set up by the ECD, whose members were all men. The EDC itself had one woman member out of a total of sixteen.

38 *Women's Two Roles: Home and Work*, A. Myrdal and V. Klein, Routledge and Kegan Paul, 2nd ed., 1968.

39 A. Hunt, *A Survey of Women's Employment*, HMSO, 1968.

40 *A Career for Women in Industry?* by Nancy Seear, Veronica Roberts and John Brock, Oliver and Boyd Ltd, for the London School of Economics, 1964.

41 *Women at Work* by Pauline Pinder, PEP Broadsheet 512, 1969.

Chapter 3

42 The campaign for ERA has also become popularly, though inaccurately, identified with the struggle for liberal abortion laws. Abortion as of right is one of the classic demands of women's liberation. In Europe, there is wide popular support for liberal abortion laws, and the opposition stems from religious organizations.

43 The expression 'women's lib' itself, with its contemptuous abbreviation, is a form of denigration. No-one refers to 'Palestinian Lib' or 'lib for Zimbabwe'.

44 I have never understood what 'femininity 'means: it is clearly very important to some people. Is it a genteel way of saying 'sex appeal'?

Chapter 4

45 Sources – *Woman in Sweden in the light of statistics* published by the Joint Female Labour Council, 1973; Annika Baude unpublished paper 'Public Policy and Changing Family Patterns in Sweden 1930–1977'.

46 Source – Female Activity Rates – Department of Employment Gazette, January 1974.

47 Source – A Profile of Women in Scotland – Board for Information on Youth and Community Service, 1976.

48 49 Source – Women and Employment in the United Kingdom, Ireland and Denmark, R. B. Cornu, EEC, 1974 (quoting official UK figures, p. 2).

50 The economic slowdown and women's employment opportunities Diane Werneke – International Labour Review, Vol. 117, No. 1, January–February 1978.

51 *Improving Job Opportunities for Women – A Chartbook Focusing on the Progress in Business*, Ruth G. Shaeffer and Helen Axel, The Conference Board, New York, 1978.

52 Information about pension arrangements is contained in Annex 3 (Overseas Practice) to a note on Equal Status for Men and Women in Occupational Pension Schemes issued by the Occupation Pensions Board, London in April 1975.

53 Conference Board analysis quoted by Stewart Fleming in a *Financial Times* article on 15 May 1978.

Chapter 5

54 European Social Charter, Council of Europe, Strasbourg, 'Council of Europe activities to further women's interests', Strasbourg, 1975.

55 Churchill Fellow Research Report on equal opportunity in North America 'Right On, Sister!', published privately, 1976.

56 Price V. Civil Service Commission. An account of this case is given in the British Equal Opportunities Commission's Second Annual Report, 1977 at pages 17–18.

57 See articles by Goodman and Novarra cited in bibliography.

58 'Anti-Discrimination Legislation', article by Julie Richter in 'Women and Labour Conference' papers, Macquarie University, 1978.

[59] See my report 'Right On, Sister!' listed in bibliography, Chapter 4 and Appendix 6.

[60] Extracted from a paper presented by Mr Kofke at a seminar held by the Aspen Institute, Berlin, September 1978, under the title 'The Dilemma of Women: Homemaking vs Career?'

[61] The judgement is quoted at length in Ruth G. Shaeffer's *Non Discrimination in Employment 1973–1975*, Conference Board, New York, 1975.

[62] The official Committee on Equality between Men and Women in Sweden has put forward a draft law under which employers would have a duty actively to work towards equality. This proposal owes much to the United States affirmative action system.

[63] See Dr E. M. Byrne's report for EEC listed in bibliography.

Chapter 6

[64] On 8 February 1979, the *Guardian* reprinted from *Socialist Challenge* an account by a young women of her four-year apprenticeship as an electrician installer. She was sworn at, hit and ostracised by the men. One is reminded of the male medical students who subjected the first women students to vile abuse and slammed the gates of Surgeon's Hall, Edinburgh in their faces. That was in 1870.

An able young woman in my office, who describes herself as 'working class', read the *Guardian* extract and commented that 'you could understand why they didn't want her there', but hitting her was too much. Women's ability to empathize is not always an advantage!

[65] See Audrey Hunt's survey of management attitudes to women. Published in 1975, this revealed some incredibly archaic and prejudiced views on the part of British managers. See also Seear and others, op. cit.

[66] 'Schlemiel' is someone who has more than the ordinary share of misfortunes and setbacks.

[67] It has gone down to legend that Joyce Butler, MP introduced the first British Sex Discrimination Bill because she found out that a woman conductor had applied for an inspector's job, only to be told that you had to have done bus driving before you could be an inspector. When the applicant expressed willingness to

drive a bus, if this was the promotion route, she was told that only men could be drivers.

68 Britain's first Act limiting factory hours was passed to protect orphan children. Later parents objected to introduction of compulsory schooling because it deprived them of a source of income.

69 See Shorter, *The Making of the Modern Family*, Chapter Five, especially pp. 191–6.

70 Leeson and Gray, op. cit., p. 34.

71 See Novarra, *Right On, Sister!*, p. 72.

SELECT BIBLIOGRAPHY

Particulars of most of the publications I have cited are given in the relevant Notes and References. In this bibliography I repeat those references under alphabetical listing and also add the titles of other works which I have used or which may be of interest to any reader who wants to delve further into a particular topic. I have not attempted to list the numerous books, pamphlets, reports, statutes, conference papers, press cuttings and ephemera which have also formed part of the background to this book.

Where a work has been published in Britain and the United States I have, where applicable, given the reference to the publication in both countries.

BAUDE, Annika
Public Policy and Changing Family Patterns in Sweden, 1930–1977, translated by Jeanne Rose, unpublished paper

BERNSTEIN, Marcelle
Nuns, Collins, 1976; Lippincott, 1976; Fount Paperbacks, 1978

BYRNE, Eileen M.
Equality of education and training for girls in the second level of education, Commission of the European Communities, 1978
Women and Education, Tavistock, 1978

Dr Bryne's studies are important in showing that unless major changes are made in the education system, girls and women will not be equipped to take advantage of equal opportunities

CHIPLIN, Brian and SLOANE, Peter J.
Sex Discrimination in the Labour Market, Macmillan, 1976

CORNU, R. B.
Women and Employment in the United Kingdom, Ireland and Denmark, Commission of the European Communities, 1974

COUNCIL OF EUROPE
Council of Europe Activities to further women's interests 1975, European Social Charter

Resolutions of the Committee of Ministers containing recommendations in the social field 1977

DAVIES, Julia
A Study of Hospital Management Training in its Organizational Context, Centre for Business Research in association with Manchester Business School, University of Manchester, 1972

DINNERSTEIN, Dorothy
The Rocking of the Cradle and the Ruling of the World, Souvenir Press, 1978

The author attacks the myth that mothers are best suited to look after children and makes a strong plea for equal parenthood for fathers

ECONOMIC DEVELOPMENT COUNCIL FOR THE CLOTHING INDUSTRY
Labour Turnover, National Economic Development Council, 1967

EDMUNDS, Lynne
Should Wives Be Paid for doing Housework?, Woman's Journal, March 1978

FOX, Alan
A Sociology of Work in Industry, Collier-Macmillan, 1971

FRIEDAN, Betty
The Feminine Mystique, Victor Gollancz, 1963; Norton, 1963

GALBRAITH, J. K.
Economics and the Public Purpose, Houghton Mifflin, 1974; Andre Deutsch, 1974

GHEZ, Gilbert R. and BECKER, Gary S.
The Allocation of Time and Goods over the Life Cycle, National Bureau of Economic Research, Columbia University Press, 1975

GILBRETH, Frank and Lilian
The Writings of the Gilbreths, ed. Spriegel and Myers, Richard D. Irwin, 1953

GOODMAN, Janet S. and NOVARRA, Virginia
The Sex Discrimination Act 1975 – a role for psychologists, Bulletin

of the British Psychological Society (1977) 30, 104–105

The Sex Discrimination Act 1975 – File and Forget?, Personnel Review, Vol. 7, No. 1, Winter 1978

HARTNETT, Oonagh
Affirmative Action Programmes, Women Speaking, April–June 1976

HENNIG, Margaret and JARDIM, Anne
The Managerial Woman, Anchor/Doubleday, 1977; Marion Boyars, 1978

A best seller in the USA. An excellent study based on extensive research and practical experience.

HUNT, Audrey
Management Attitudes and Practices Towards Women at Work, Office of Population Censuses and Surveys, 1975
A Survey of Women's Employment, HMSO, 1968

HUTTON, John
The Mystery of Wealth, Stanley Thornes (Publishers) Limited, 1978

A useful introduction to the history and development of economic ideas

JAY, Anthony
Corporation Man, Jonathan Cape, 1972
Management and Machiavelli, Hodder and Stoughton, 1967; Holt, Rinehart & Winston Inc., 1968

JEPHCOTT, Pearl with SEEAR, Nancy and SMITH, John H.
Married Women Working, George Allen and Unwin, 1962

JOINT FEMALE LABOUR COUNCIL, SWEDEN
The Woman in Sweden in the Light of Statistics, Arbetsmarknadens Kvinnonämnd, 1973

KAHN, Hilda, with KOHEN, Andrew I.
Economic Perspectives on the Roles of Women in the American Economy, Journal of Economic Literature, 13 December 1975, pp. 1249–92
Also available as a Radcliffe Reprint

LEESON, Joyce and GRAY, Judith
Women in Medicine, Tavistock, 1978

LEWENHAK, Sheila
Women and Trade Unions, Ernest Benn Limited, 1977

LILJESTROM, Rita, MELLSTROM, Gunilla F. and SVENSSON, Gillian L.
Sex Roles in Transition: A Report on a Pilot Program in Sweden,
Advisory Council to the Prime Minister on Equality between
Men and Women, 1975

An account of the scheme for introducing women into 'men's jobs' in
Kristianstad County

MACKIE, Lindsay and PATTULLO, Polly
Women at Work, Tavistock, 1977

MANT, Alistair
The Rise and Fall of the British Manager, Macmillan, 1977

MATTFIELD, Jacquelyn A. and VAN AKEN, Carol G. (ed.)
Women and the Scientific Professions, Massachusetts Institute of
Technology Press, 1965

ALFRED MARKS BUREAU LIMITED
*A Survey of the Opinions, Problems and Achievements of Women in
Senior Management*, Statistical Services Division, Alfred Marks
Bureau Limited, 1977

MITCHELL, Juliet
Women's Estate, Penguin Books, 1971; Random House, 1973

MORGAN, Elaine
Falling Apart: The Rise and Decline of Urban Civilization, Souvenir
Press, 1976; Stein & Day, 1977; Abacus Sphere Books, 1978

MORGAN, Robin (ed.)
Sisterhood is Powerful, an anthology of writings from the women's
liberation movement, Vintage Books, Random House, New
York, 1970

MORRIS, Joan
*Against Nature and God: The History of Women with the Jurisdiction
of Bishops*, Macmillan, 1973 (under the title *The Lady was a
Bishop*); Mowbrays, 1974

MYRDAL, A. and KLEIN, V.
Women's Two Roles: Home and Work, Routledge and Kegan Paul,
2nd ed., 1968; Humanities Press Inc., 1970

NIVEN, Mary
Personnel Management 1913–1963, Institute of Personnel Management, 1967

NOVARRA, Virginia
Right On, Sister!, report on Churchill Fellowship research on equal opportunity for women in North America, published privately, 1976

OAKLEY, Ann
The Sociology of Housework, Martin Robertson, 1974; Pantheon Books, 1975

OECD
Employment of Women: Report on Regional Trade Union, Seminar, 1968, OECD, Paris, 1970

PELLING, Henry
A History of British Trade Unionism, Penguin Books, 2nd ed., 1971; St Martin's Press Inc., 1977

PIGOU, A. C.
The Economics of Welfare, Macmillan, 4th ed., 1962; AMS Press Inc., 1976; reprints of 4th ed. of 1932

PINDER, Pauline
Women at Work, PEP Broadsheet 512, 1969

PUGH, D. S. (ed.)
Organization Theory, Penguin Modern Management Readings, 1971

PUGH, D. S., HICKSON, D. J. and HININGS, C. R.
Writers on Organizations, Penguin Modern Management Texts, 2nd ed., 1971
Contains chapters on Mary P. Follett, Jane S. Mouton and Joan Woodward

RAPOPORT, Rhona and Robert
Dual Career Families, Pelican, 1971

ROWBOTHAM, Sheila
Women, Resistance and Revolution, Pantheon Books, 1973; Penguin, 1974

SAMUELSON, Paul A.
Economics, McGraw-Hill, 10th ed., 1976

SCHREINER, Olive
Women and Labour, 1911, reprinted Virago Limited, 1978; reprinted Johnson Reprint Corp. and Gordon Press Pubs.
A classic which still has relevance today

SCHULTZ, Theodore W. (ed.)
Economics of the Family, National Bureau of Economic Research, University of Chicago Press, 1973

SCOTTISH PROJECTS COMMITTEE
A Profile of Women in Scotland, International Women's Year Scottish Projects Committee, 1975

SEEAR, Nancy, ROBERTS, Veronica and BROCK, John
A Career for Women in Industry?, Oliver and Boyd Limited for London School of Economics, 1964

SEELAND, Suzanne
Equal Opportunities and Vocational Training, report of a Seminar held in Berlin in 1977, European Centre for the Development of Vocational Training, Berlin, 1978

SHAEFFER, Ruth G.
Non-discrimination in Employment: Changing Perspectives 1963–1972, Conference Board, New York, 1973
Non-discrimination in Employment 1973–1975 A Broadening and Deepening National Effort, Conference Board, New York, 1975

Ruth Shaeffer's work is highly recommended to those who wish to study the technical problems of equal opportunity programmes. She is continuing her research into the implementation of equal opportunity in the private sector in the United States.

SHAEFFER, Ruth G. and AXEL, Helen
Improving Job Opportunities for Women: A Chartbook Focusing on the Progress in Business, Conference Board, New York, 1978

SHORTER, Edward
The Making of the Modern Family, Basic Books Inc., 1975; Collins 1976; Fontana, 1977

This work is particularly useful because it draws its source material from many different countries

STEAD, Bette Anne
Women's Contributions to Management Thought, Business Horizons, February 1974

STENDHAL
De l'Amour, 1822, translation by Gilbert and Suzanne Sale issued under the title *Love* in Penguin Classics, 1975; French and European Publications Inc., 1959

This book contains some interesting observations on the education of women

TECHNOLOGY, Ministry of
Woman, Wife and Worker, (summary of part of Jephcott's work qv.), 1960, in association with the Social Science Department of the London School of Economics

TIGER, Lionel and SHEPHER, Joseph
Women in the Kibbutz, Harcourt Brace Jovanovich Inc., 1975; Penguin Books, 1977

TOLSON, Andrew
The Limits of Masculinity, Tavistock, 1977

This book gives an account of men's response to the women's movement and their search for their own liberation

TUCKWELL, G. M. and others
Women in Industry from Seven Points of View, Duckworth, 1908

TURNBULL, P. and WILLIAMS G.
Sex Differentials in Teachers' Pay, unpublished study for the Higher Education Research Unit

WERNEKE, Diane
The Economic Slowdown and Women's Employment Opportunities, International Labour Review, Volume 117, No. 1, January–February 1978

WILD, R. and HILL, A. B.
Women In the Factory: A Study of Job Satisfaction and Labour Turnover, Institute of Personnel Management, 1970

WOMEN AND LABOUR CONFERENCE
Conference Papers published by the Convenors of the Conference, 1978, School of History, Philosophy and Politics, Macquarie University, New South Wales

A treasure trove of information about the Australian women's movement past and present with many interesting and scholarly papers